The Divine Library

[illegible]

સ્વરગમાં રેહવીવાલા અમારા બાપ તારૂં નામ પવિત્ર

नमो नारायणाय ॥ ओं यस्परस्मरणमात्रे ण जन्मसंसारब

ས་ཀྱི་ཡབ་ནམ་མཁའི་གློང་དུ་བཞུགས་པའི། ཁྱེད་ཀྱི་མཚན་ཐམས་ཅད་ཀྱིས་

আমারদের স্বর্গস্থ পিতা তোমার নাম পবিত্র মান্য

ଆମ୍ଭମାନଙ୍କର ସ୍ୱର୍ଗସ୍ଥ ପିତା ତୁମ୍ଭର ନାମ ପବିତ୍ର ମାନ୍ୟ ହେଉ ।

යෙහි වැඩසිටින අපගේ පියානන්වහන්ස ඔබවහන්සේගේ නාමය සු

ളുടെ സ്വർഗ്ഗസ്ഥനായ പിതാവെ നിന്റെ നാമം പരിശുദ്ധമാക്കപ്പെടെ

ငါ့ အဘ ပိတာ တဝ နာမော ပဝိတ္တော ဟောတု ။

[illegible]

ԱՆԷ էր բանն. և բանն էր առ ա՛ծ. և ա՛ծ էր բանն: Նա՛ էր ի սկզբանէ առ

ო- ჩუენო: რომელი: ხარ: ცათა: შინა: წმიდა: იყავნ: სა

ἡμῶν, ὁ ἐν τοῖς οὐρανοῖς, ἁγιασθήτω τὸ ὄνομά σου.

ο ἡμῶν ὁ ἐν τοῖς οὐρανοῖς ἁγιασθήτω τὸ ὄνομά σου

𐌿𐌽𐍃𐌰𐍂 𐌸𐌿 𐌹̈𐌽 𐌷𐌹𐌼𐌹𐌽𐌰𐌼: 𐍅𐌴𐌹𐌷𐌽𐌰𐌹 𐌽𐌰𐌼𐍉 𐌸𐌴𐌹𐌽·

[illegible]

НАШЬ ИЖЕ ѤСИ НА НЕБСЕХЪ. ДА СТИТЬСѦ ИМѦ

нашъ, сущій на небесахъ! Да святится имя Твое.

е нашъ, сущій на небесахъ! Да святится им

unsir. du in himile bist. din namo werde giheiliget

unser der du bist im himel. Geheiliget werde dein name.

The Divine Library

**A COMPREHENSIVE REFERENCE GUIDE
TO THE SACRED TEXTS AND
SPIRITUAL LITERATURE OF THE WORLD**

Rufus C. Camphausen

Inner Traditions International
Rochester, Vermont

Inner Traditions International, Ltd.
One Park Street
Rochester, Vermont 05767

LIBRARY OF CONGRESS CATALOGING-IN-PUBLICATION DATA
Camphausen, Rufus C.
    The divine library: a comprehensive reference guide to the sacred texts and spiritual literature of the world / Rufus C. Camphausen.
        p. cm.
    Includes bibliographical references and index.
    ISBN 0-89281-351-2
    1. Sacred books—History and criticsm. 2. Religious literature—History and criticsm.
I. Title.
BL71.C36 1992
291.8'2–dc20   91–39547
                                                                                          CIP

Printed and bound in the United States

10 9 8 7 6 5 4 3 2 1

Distributed to the book trade in the United States by American International Distribution Corporation (AIDC)
Distributed to the book trade in Canada by Book Center, Inc., Montreal, Quebec

Text Design by Virginia L. Scott

Illustration credits:
Page 59 from Chakras by Harish Johari (Destiny Books, Rochester, Vt., 1987).
Page 70 by Shirley Triest, from Mahabharata by William Buck, © 1973 The Regents of the University of California (University of California Press, Berkeley and Los Angeles, 1973).
Page 92 reproduced with permission of the British Library, Oriental and India Office Collections (8219 P2).
Pages 125 and 129 by Robert Beer, from Masters of Enchantment by Keith Dowman (Inner Traditions International, Rochester, Vt., 1988).
Page 133 from The Tibetan Book of the Dead by W. Y. Evans-Wentz (Oxford University Press, New York and London, 3rd ed., 1960).
Pages 139 and 149 from Tools for Tantra by Harish Johari (Inner Traditions International, Rochester, Vt., 1986).
Page 141 from Breath, Mind, and Consciousness by Harish Johari (Destiny Books, Rochester, Vt., 1989).
Pages 160–161 from Zen Flesh, Zen Bones by Paul Reps (Charles E. Tuttle Co., Tokyo, Japan, 1975).
Page 169 reproduced with permission of The Brinton Collection, Dept. of Special Collections, Van Pelt-Dietrich Library Center, University of Pennsylvania.

to Christina, whose love and warmth sustain and encourage me

———————————————————————◆———————————————————————

I would like to take this opportunity to express my appreciation to publisher Ehud Sperling and the all-female staff he has gathered at Inner Traditions. Without the professional efforts and truly mindful assistance of this team, The Divine Library *would not have become what it is. Special thanks go to art director Estella Arias for her final choices concerning the cover, and to editor Jeanie Levitan for being my warm and friendly "literary midwife."*

Contents

Preface

In order to best undertake a survey of the world's sacred texts and spiritual literature, both author and reader should do their utmost to muster a degree of emotional detachment, intellectual relativity, and critical objectivity. Simultaneously, a certain degree of respect is necessary, again from both sides, for the concepts and thoughts of all cultures, of all religious schools and systems, and for their members.

We would do well to realize that the wide diversity of myths and legends, morals and rituals that speak from the pages of the world's religious and spiritual literature are the work of inspired men and women. The texts, whether "received," "inspired," or "channeled," are the work of all-too-human beings, neighbors of ours in time, all of whom were guided and motivated by the truly human need and desire to understand self and other, world and universe, birth and death—and the incredibly wide spectrum of phenomena between Heaven and Earth.

Certain cultural concepts, problems and solutions, theories and practices may sound strange to us, perhaps primitive or ignorant. Yet judging them too quickly, from within our own particular and restricted cultural backgrounds—however enlightened and tolerant our own mind-set may seem to us—will deny us true understanding and limit our access to the *condition humain* that underlies the existential problems of all humanity.

Religious systems come and go, as do societies and cultures, values, visions, and dreams. Just as with individuals like you and me, religions too are subject to the Wheel of Time; they are born, mature, grow old, and most often eventually cease to exist—some sooner, others later. The fact that a few religious systems have persisted much longer than others does not in itself indicate that they were, or are, intrinsically better or more advanced; it merely indicates that they were helped to stay and to last by individuals and groups. All too often this type of survival, of winners who therefore seem to represent the One Truth, has been dependent on totally nonreligious and nonspiritual grounds. Individual power struggles, politics, wars, the suppression of other beliefs—much human suffering and the shedding of oceans of blood—have often accompanied and motivated the survival of those creeds that have come to be called world religions.

Most readers will have at least heard of some works associated with these religions: the Vedas and Upanishads of classical Hinduism, the Torah and Talmud of Judaism, the New Testament of the Christian Bible, the Islamic Qur'an, and, perhaps, the Pali Canon or the Kanjur of Buddhism. These few constitute only the very major works of the largest religions still active and more or less alive today.

Once we take a closer look at the rich heritage of similar sacred scriptures that have been written throughout human history, each of those named above becomes simply one among many. They do not, of course, lose their special value to our understanding of the world, in the past as well as today; yet once we recognize them as expressions of relativity, we gain a new perspective that makes it possible to see them as beacons of light among these other equals.

It cannot be the aim of a concise reference guide such as this to achieve completeness, to describe *all* of humanity's sacred scriptures. Not only are there too many by far, but—even in the twentieth century—there are also a number that have not as yet been put into writing or have not been translated. And still others have yet to be discovered.

The Divine Library aims at introducing the reader to a broad spectrum of sacred texts, many of which are available in public libraries and bookstores across the world, by providing a historical overview of the texts' origins and laying the groundwork for further individual reading. This guide can function as a catalog to an imaginary library, whether that library actually exists in some exclusive chamber or simply exists in the mind of an interested and curious individual. The latter, of course, is quite valid, as this is the manner in which generations of humans have preserved their particular traditions before they were ever put into writing.

A large number of cultures have never produced written texts, even in traditions that still survive and are still active in present times. The great variety of tribal peoples surviving in rain forests or on reservations in North and South America, in the deserts of Australia, and in the hills, mountains, and islands of Southeast Asia all have valuable and fascinating traditions that nonetheless are rarely available as a body of scriptures and therefore—unfortunately—cannot be included in our overview. Information concerning such oral traditions can still be gathered only by actual traveling and listening or from secondary literature.

The spellings of foreign names and terms used in this book are those most commonly found in English-based publications to allow the reader to approximate the original pronunciations as closely as possible.

What we call footprints were of course produced by feet, but they are not actually the feet. In the same way, books were written by sages, but they are not the sages.
                              Ko Hung (284–364) in his Nei P'ing

"Everything has already been said!" says the cynic. And the optimist answers: "But nobody has as yet listened."
                              Dutch comedian Freek de Jonge
                              in an oral performance

The Venerable Way is not difficult at all, it only abhors picking and choosing.
                              the sixth-century Hsin-hsin-ming

Introduction

The Oral Tradition:
Our Primal Source of Wisdom

In today's world, we have come to depend to a high degree on reading and writing. Consequently, we have also come to consider literacy not only as normal for any slightly educated member of society but as a necessary prerequisite for any civilization. Some people even equate literacy with intelligence, a remnant attitude of earlier centuries when Occidental chauvinism was prevalent even more than it is today. Such a prejudice regards a culture that is not literate as un(der)developed, less civilized, lower, and its collective knowledge and wisdom is then judged as primitive, backward, and worthless—as "superstition."

Studies in anthropology, ethnology, and comparative religion, however, have by now shown clearly that all of the essential myths, and the "seed wisdom" of the later and present "high religions," were once developed and carried through time by nonliterate peoples, by means of a purely oral tradition. This is the case with the Vedas as well as with the Book of Genesis, with the I Ching and the Popol Vuh, the Epic of Gilgamesh, and many more of the classical texts.

Such preliterate and oral tradition can be detected at the root of all or most of the sacred texts we now possess in writing. Therefore, the historical period for a given text's formation, most often oral and preliterate, is usually very different—if it is known at all—from the dates of its actual compilation in writing (codification) and differs even more substantially from the time of formal acceptance and recognition of a given tradition as a holy scripture (canonization).

Time and again in history, teachings have warned against any fixation of the living, organic, changeable, oral, and largely experiential mystery traditions; some teachers and schools simply forbade putting the "secret" in writing. Perhaps the peoples most dedicated to this ancient law, and certainly the most radical in approaching this problem, are the Australian Aborigines. According to Robert Lawler's recent study *Voices of the First Day,* these people consciously rejected writing and similar manifestations of what in the West is generally regarded as progress.

The trap of fixing in writing the most complex, archetypal, and individual experiences, visions, and inspirations, however useful it may be in other areas of life, lies in creating the possibility for pure lip service, for "believing" instead of experiencing and knowing. Teachings once codified, canonized, and serially reproduced can easily become hollow and stagnant and, after a few centuries or millennia, can become devoid of their original intentions. At this point, pure obeisance to authority will be required and peoples' lives will become dictated by set interpretations of immutable scriptures.

The One Truth:
The Supremacy of Each and All Teachings

Today's five so-called major world religions—a biased and misleading term found in almost any general work on religions—must be recognized, as mentioned earlier, as Darwinian survivors. Generally speaking, these systems of belief, or schools of thought, were those smart enough, and often aggressive enough, to dominate or replace those of the nations and cultures sacked and occupied by their political and/or spiritual rulers. Despite this historical fact, however, few or none of these religious systems have truly avoided the all-too-human fallacy of claiming the absolute supremacy or "higher value" of their specific creed.

Judaism, Hinduism, Christianity, Islam, and even officially nonmissionary and declaredly nonviolent Buddhism—all these high religions have at one time or another forced their value system on peoples with other beliefs, required worship and veneration of their own specific deities, and forced their particular view of "good" and "bad" onto others. In this way, they more or less successfully fought and attempted to suppress such religious systems as Bön, Jaina, Shakta, Sufism, Gnosticism, and Zoroastrianism, as well as Indian, Tibetan, or Japanese Tantra and most of the early goddess-oriented religions of Europe, Egypt, Greece, and Mesopotamia—not to mention the innumerable preliterate, traditional, and tribal religions of all continents.

In many cases, local temples and sanctuaries were desecrated and destroyed. Sacred scriptures were stolen and suppressed, perhaps even burned to ashes. All of course was done in the name of god—be it Zeus, Jehovah, Allah, or the Lord—and his all-embracing love for his children everywhere.

It is almost miraculous, but certainly fortunate, that today we still do have so many diverse scriptures available, from so many ages and continents. We are thus able to read and study these texts, which enables us virtually to travel in time. In doing so, and in "reading between the lines," our genetic memories may invoke a time when we sat around the fire and listened to what the shaman sang, to what the medicine woman passed on, to what the priestess taught.

Study of comparative religion and mythology should not be left to theologians and historians only. For anyone, it is an interesting and rewarding pursuit, a personal odyssey into humanity's collective consciousness. Such inner time travel should not be viewed cynically as a "regressive" matter of dreaming of a life earlier and elsewhere. In making such mental journeys through time and space we are able to learn, and to better grasp, all that is essentially human: birth and death, love and fear, joy and ecstasy, dreaming and experiencing visionary insights into the fields of energy that continuously unfold and manifest as universe and life.

Books have been burned quite frequently in human history, as in this scene from the destruction of the Alexandria Library.

Of Canons, Hidden Texts, and the Burning of Books

Most religious systems of belief, once they possess a number of texts that represent the groups' teachings, have attempted to establish an official canon. Usually a body of priests will hold council and decide which of the works are regarded as divine revelations, which as authentic sayings of the particular group's founder, and which as "true" and "valuable" interpretation and exegetical material. In the process, other works will be declared uninspired, second-class material, "false teaching" or heresy, or attempts to mislead others. This process has occurred, to name but the best-known examples, in early Judaism (see **Apocrypha and Pseudepigrapha**) and Christianity (see **Apocryphic Gospels**), in Buddhism (see **Kanjur, Tripitaka**), in Islam (see **Hadith**), and in early Hinduism (see **Atharva Veda**).

Such canonization, of course, can be upheld only if there is a continuous religio-political body of authority that is able to censor and decree, then prosecute and punish, any derivation from the desired norm. In this regard, the various religious systems differ not only in their strictness, but also in their outlook concerning change; they differ in their encouragement of, or resistance against, valuable renewing impulses. The most authoritarian systems, the three competing Near Eastern creeds of Judaism, Christianity, and Islam, have early on fixed their canons strongly and rigidly; never has any new development been allowed to gain the status of "sacred scripture." For this reason, these religions claim little space in humanity's Divine Library.

On the other hand, systems such as Hinduism and Buddhism have been forced to adapt, have allowed for a much more dynamic stance, or both. Within the fold of these religions, major developments have led to newer canons, coexisting with older scriptures, that have become equally important and gained equally sacred or high spiritual status.

A unique way of making sure that a living tradition does not become stale, dry out, and ultimately die was introduced by Padmasambhava (c. 717– c. 804), traditionally regarded as the major figure to have introduced Buddhism into Tibet. With deep knowledge of human nature,

Padmasambhava established a spiritual tradition of so-called treasures (in Tibetan called *termas*), "hidden texts" that were to be found at some point in the future by *tertons,* well-trained, wise, and initiated "revealers of treasures."

The tradition was based in the very real and practical need to hide actual texts and teachings from those who endeavored to suppress and outlaw early Vajrayana, the Tibetan branch of Buddhism. Padmasambhava raised this hide-and-seek game to a higher, immaterial or magical, level. Along with literally hiding actual books or scrolls, he and the Lady Yeshe Tsogyal (c. 757– c. 817), his most trusted female partner, took to "hiding" their teachings outside of material reality, encoded in the "twilight language" spoken in the divine spheres. Such magically protected teachings were, in other words, deposited in the spheres of the collective mind and cosmic consciousness. At least, the teachers put out the word that this is what they had done, and they predicted that these *termas* would be rediscovered by certain *tertons* in the future. And so they were—and still are. Regularly, and well into the twentieth century, a number of Tibetan texts appeared that are said to represent such long-lost treasures of ancient wisdom, the "found" and "rediscovered" teachings of the ancient masters. Thus well-cared-for, the sacred literature is kept alive and growing.

Other works, however, from other cultures and religious schools, truly have been lost forever. These works have actually been hunted down, forbidden, trampled upon, and most often burned to ashes. A detailed study of suppressed, destroyed, and burned books would fill an entire volume; here it suffices to say that members of the most varied religious and cultural backgrounds have committed this cultural crime against freedom and against humanity as a whole. A number of such incidents have been incorporated in the Wheel of Time outlined below and are sometimes discussed with the relevant texts.

The Wheel of Time

A Note on Dating the Texts

With few exceptions, the dating of ancient texts and their authors is a tedious and difficult task. This is especially so when the texts originated in cultures that placed less significance on such information than we might, and also holds true with texts from so-called prehistoric times of which we have little or no written record. The dates given in *The Divine Library*'s Wheel of Time have been researched and cross-checked as much as possible, although quandaries remain in those instances in which even members of the established scientific community do not agree with one another.

Wherever possible, such inconsistencies and disagreements have been noted—for example in the case of the Persian prophet Zarathushtra (Zoroaster) or the Chinese sage Lao-tzu—rather than giving personal preference to one or another particular theory. On the other hand, the temporal layout of the present work, designed to allow for a developmental rather than cultural or ethnic overview, and with an extra focus on the oral tradition beyond all written scriptures, has resulted in historical data sometimes quite different from that given in conservative historical works or general encyclopedias.

If, for example, there are clear indications that a written, codified, and canonized work contains oral traditions much older than any of the available written manuscripts, *The Divine Library* gives precedence to the period of oral origin. A good example of this development from oral poems and hymns to a written version of the tradition can be found in the Egyptian Pyramid Texts, the spiritually inspired funerary documents that have come to us in the form of hieroglyphs chiseled into the walls of pyramids of the fifth dynasty (2494–2345 B.C.E.). This literal "writing on the wall" occurred almost immediately after the invention of a written language in Egypt, which occurred in the period 3000–2500 B.C.E. The contents of these texts, however, show clearly—and here most scientists do agree—that their origins are in the orally transmitted traditions of Egypt's so-called predynastic past, the vast period between 5000 B.C.E. and 3100 B.C.E.

Based on such information, several of the sacred texts presented here have thus been dated much earlier than general consensus—usually conservative and requiring "solid evidence" (i.e., written documents)—would allow. This method has nonetheless been used mainly for the period of time before the common era (B.C.E.). Once literacy had been solidly established in most of the cultures that produced written texts at all, the historical chart will show dates of authors or existing manuscripts rather than always referring back to the most ancient source of the teachings. It makes no sense, for example, to date an inspired text, clearly written and published by an eleventh-century master, to the historical time of the Buddha. If, in the Wheel of Time, a certain date is said to be "generally accepted," this phrase is meant to indicate that scholars and scientists generally agree on this dating. Use of the term "traditional," however, indicates that members and publications of the cultural tradition itself give precedence to that particular date.

Abbreviations

~ = approximate date

b. = born (year of birth)

B.C.E. = before the common era

c. = circa

C.E. = common era

Chin. = Chinese

d. = died (year of death)

Jap. = Japanese

Skt. = *Sanskrit

Tib. = Tibetan

All terms in boldface type refer to scriptures discussed in the main part of the book. Any term marked with an asterisk (*) is an entry in the glossary.

A note regarding Chinese titles: In order to facilitate the reader's recognition of titles and terms in other works of classical sinological studies, Chinese titles have not been given in the modern Pinyin transliteration, but in the much better known and more often used Wade-Giles system. Pinyin (Chinese, "phonetic spelling") is a script adopted by the Chinese government in 1958 that renders Chinese ideograms in a romanized phonetic alphabet of fifty-eight letters. Although Pinyin is slowly gaining acceptance for use in publications such as encyclopedias and newspapers, terms such as Ha shang (for *Mahayana Buddhism) and Zhang Zhung (the early Tibetan kingdom) are much more recognizable than their modern Pinyin equivalents, Haxan and Xanxun.

The Wheel of Time 5000 B.C.E.–the Present

A Historical Overview of Scriptures, Authors, Prophets, Sages, and Related Cultural Events

◆

5th and 4th millennia B.C.E.

period of preliterate formation of the I Ching (see also
    Chinese Classics) and the Egyptian Pyramid Texts
3201   beginning of the *Kali Yuga

3rd millennium B.C.E.

3000–2500 ~time for the invention of Egyptian hieroglyphs
    ~date for the beginning development of Chinese ideograms
    ~date for undeciphered texts of the Indus Valley
      civilization; first evidence for proto-yoga (see 800 B.C.E.)
    ~date for Enoch/Henoch
    ~period of preliterate formation of the Cycle of Inanna
      (Sumer) and the Gilgamesh Epos (Sumer)
2953–2838 conservative dates for the emperor Fu Hsi (China) and his
    early version of the I Ching

2700	Gilgamesh possibly the ruler of Uruk, Sumer
2494–2345	Egyptian fifth dynasty with stone-incised **Pyramid Texts**
2300	cuneiform writing in Sumer
2300–1000	period of time covered by the Shu Ching (**Chinese Classics**)
2133–1991	Egyptian eleventh dynasty with the first **Coffin Texts**

2nd millennium B.C.E.

2000–1900	~date for the patriarch Abraham
2000–1450	Minoan civilization flourishes on Crete
1800	cuneiform writing in Babylonia
	~date for the **Enuma Elish**
1792	Mesopotamian ruler and lawmaker Hammurabi ascends to throne of Babylon
1760	~date for the **Gilgamesh Epos** (Sumer, Babylon)
1750	~date for the **Cycle of Inanna** (Sumer)
1600	~date for the first texts of the Egyptian **Book of the Ever Deathless**
1550–1450	~date for the preliterate formation of the **Rig Veda, Sama Veda,** and **Yajur Veda** (India)
1500	cuneiform writing among the Hittites
	probable time for the Persian prophet Zarathushtra (in Greek known as Zoroaster) and for his **Gathas**
	preliterate formation of the **Avesta**
1500–1350	~date for Moses
1411	~date for the Egyptian Hymns to the Sun God, based on the **Pyramid Texts**
1411–1397	reign of Pharaoh Thutmose IV (Egypt)
1200	~date for beginning of Jahweh worship (Judaism), oral formation of texts that make up the Torah and the **Old Testament**
1194	the fall of Troy, giving rise to the preliterate formation of the **Iliad** and **Odyssey**
1191	birth of King Wen

1160	~date of birth for the Duke of Chou
1143	date for the I Ching of King Wen and the Duke of Chou (China, *Taoism)
1010–962	~date for King David

1st millennium B.C.E.

1000	~date for the preliterate formation of the Atharva Veda (India)
	~date for the oldest traditions represented in the Tao-tsang
1000–500	originating period for the Shih Ching (Chinese Classics)
990–922	King Solomon
950	~date for the preliterate formation of the Song of Songs (Judaism)
	~date for the preliterate formation of the Five Books of the Law (the Torah or Pentateuch) said to have been received by Moses, including the Ten Commandments (see Genesis and Old Testament)
900	~date for the Shatapatha Brahmana, probably the oldest of the Brahmanas
	~date for the oldest Aranyakas

8th century B.C.E.

800	~beginning of preclassical yoga, the tradition that gave rise to the Yoga Sutra
	~traditional date for the oral Tsalagi Teachings of the Cherokee Indians
800–700	~dates for the Brihad-Aranyaka Upanishad and the Chandogya Upanishad
800–400	~date for most of the Aranyakas, Brahmanas, and Upanishads
740	~date for the prophet Isaiah and thus for the Old Testament book named after him

722–481 period of the Chinese Chou Dynasty and the state of Lu; both the Li Ching and the Ch'un Ch'iu (**Chinese Classics**) cover this time

7th century B.C.E.

700 ~date for the first version Homer's **Iliad** (Greece)
~date for the biblical books Deuteronomy, Joshua, and Judges, and for the final version of the books of Samuel (**Old Testament**)
~date for preliterate formation of the **Ramayana**

664–525 period of major revisions in the Egyptian **Book of the Ever Deathless**

650 probable date for a preliterate formation of the **Tao-te Ching**

628–551 generally accepted dates for Zarathushtra/Zoroaster (see 1500 B.C.E.)

616–579 Tarquinius Priscus, an Etruscan king, purchases the **Sibylline Books**

600 ~date for a written **Rig Veda**

6th century B.C.E.

probable time for a written **Avesta**

599–527 traditional dates for the founder of *Jaina, Vardhamana/ Mahavira (see 540 B.C.E.)

597–539 period of Jewish exile in Babylonia

592–550 the prophet Ezekiel; period for the biblical books Jeremiah, Ezekiel, and Kings (**Old Testament**)

580–500 traditional dates for Lao-tzu (or Lao-tse)

563–483 Siddhartha Gautama Shakyamuni Buddha (born on April 8, 563 B.C.E.)

starting point for the historical epic **Mahavamsa** (Sri Lanka)

551–479 K'ung-tzu, or Confucius

540	earliest date for texts of the **Mahabharata** (India)
540–468	generally accepted dates for Vardhamana/Mahavira (*Jaina) (see 599 B.C.E.)
525	traditional date for the **Tao-te Ching** (China, *Taoism) (see 350 B.C.E.)
520	~date for **Old Testament** books Zechariah and Deutero-Isaiah (Isaiah 40–66, written by others)
500	~period of formation for the **Angas** (India, *Jaina)

5th century B.C.E.

	~date for written versions of **Genesis**, Exodus, and Numbers (**Old Testament**)
	~probable formation of texts known as **Orphic Hymns**
480	first Buddhist council (three years after death of Buddha)
480–390	alternative date for Lao-tzu (see 580 B.C.E.)
475	~date for the Vinaya and Sutra Pitakas (**Tripitaka**), including the **Brahmajala Sutra** (*Buddhism)
443	Rome establishes an office for censorship
409	date for earliest texts of the Lun Yü (**Confucian Canon**); seventy years after the death of K'ung-tzu (China)

4th century B.C.E.

	~date for the books Job and Proverbs (**Old Testament**)
371–289	Meng-tzu (or Mencius); author of the Meng-tzu (**Confucian Canon**)
369–286	~dates for Chuang-tzu, or Chuang Chou
350	~scientific date for **Tao-te Ching** (China, *Taoism) (see 525 B.C.E.)
	~date for a written **Song of Songs**
	~date for the **Avadhutagita**
340	~date for the Inner Chapters of the **Chuang-tzu** (China, *Taoism) (see 742 C.E.)

330 ~date for the **Lieh-tzu** (Lie-zi, Liä Dsi) (China, ★Taoism)
       Alexander destroys the old **Avesta**
300 ~date for most texts of the **Mahabharata** and for the
       Bhagavadgita (India)
       ~date for the establishment of the libraries at Alexandria and
       Pergamum as centers of learning

3rd century B.C.E.

~date for the Book of Jonah (**Old Testament**)
285 completion of the Septuagint, a Greek translation of the
       so-called Hebrew Bible (see **Old Testament**)
284–246 **Hymns to Isis at Philae** (Egypt)
250 ~date for formative work on the Abhidharma(**Tripitaka**)
       ~date for the Gnostic **Pistis Sophia** and for a written
       Tao-te Ching
247/246 third Buddhist council declares ★Theravada as official,
       orthodox ★Buddhism, and other schools as heretic
240 **Dhammapada** officially recognized as sayings of the Buddha,
       at the Council of Ashoka
213 burning of **Chinese Classics** under Emperor Ch'in Shih
       Huang Ti and revision of the Chinese written language
200 ~date for a written **Atharva Veda** (see 1000 B.C.E.)
       ~date for the Ma-wang-tui manuscripts (see **Tao-te Ching**)

2nd century B.C.E.

~date for the Confucian **I Ching** commentaries, and for the
       newly written and probably revised **Chinese Classics**
200–120 blossoming of the religious/alchemical tradition of ★Taoism,
       the oral tradition of which can be found in the later
       Nei P'ien (see 320 C.E.)
       ~date for beginning formation of the **Mishnah** (see late
       2nd/early 3rd century C.E.)

~date for the **Ashtavakra Samhita** of Ashtavakra

168   the Jewish Torah (see **Old Testament**) is forbidden and
burned under the Hellenistic king Antiochus IV Epiphanes

164   Daniel, a late book of the **Old Testament**

160   ~date for the apocryphic "Additions to Daniel," the Book of
Tobit and 1 Esdras; also for the pseudepigraphic Book of
Enoch and the Book of Jubilees (**Apocrypha and
Pseudepigraphia of the Old Testament**)

150   date for oldest **Dead Sea Scrolls** from Qumran

    ~earliest date for the **Yoga Sutra** of Patanjali (India)

1st century B.C.E.

~date for the earliest portion of the *Shiva Purana, begun late
in the 2nd century B.C.E. (see **Puranas**, 4th century C.E.)

~date for the extant **Orphic Hymns**, begun late in the
2nd century B.C.E.

~date for the Ceylonese Tipitaka (see **Tripitaka**) (*Buddhism)

~date for the **Ramayana** by Valmiki (India)

~date for 2 Esdras and the Book of Judith (**Apocrypha and
Pseudepigraphia of the Old Testament**)

86   completed version of the Shih Ching, Chinese
historical records

83   some of the **Sibylline Books** lost in fire

47   first destruction of the Alexandrian library during the
Roman siege under Julius Caesar

5–7   ~date for birth of Jesus of Nazareth

1st century B.C.E. and/or 1st century C.E.

~date for the **Prajnaparamita Sutra**, including **Diamond
Sutra** and **Heart Sutra**

~date for the preliterate formation of the material found in
the **Kojiki** and **Nihon Shoki**

1st century

~beginning date for the texts of the **Corpus Hermeticum,** lasting through the 3rd century

~beginning date for the **Avadanas,** lasting through the 3rd century

30–33 ~date for death of Jesus of Nazareth; either 3 April 30 or 7 April 33 (opinions differ)

30–96 composition of the **New Testament**

50 ~date for beginning development of *Mahayana Buddhism

50–63 the letters sent by Saul/Paulus (d. ~68 C.E.) from Rome (Colossians, Philemon, Ephesians, Philippians; **New Testament)**

60–70 Book of Matthew (**New Testament**)

60–80 Acts of the Apostles (**New Testament**)

65 earliest evidence for a Buddhist community in China

68 destruction of Qumran; last possible date for any of the **Dead Sea Scrolls**

81–96 the apocalyptic Revelation of St. John (last text of **New Testament**)

2nd century

active time of various Gnostic schools

~date for the Gospel of Mary Magdalene and other texts of **Nag Hammadi Scriptures**

100 ~date for the Synod of Jamnia (or Jabneh), during which the contents of the Hebrew Bible (see **Old Testament**) were fixed for the first time (see 325 C.E.)

100–165 ~date for Arya Nagarjuna (not the *Mahasiddha)

105 Vinaya Pitaka (**Tripitaka**) translated into Chinese (*Buddhism)

123 ~date for birth of Apuleius Lucius (Rome, b. Algeria)

135 birth of Rabbi Jehuda Ha-Nasi (Y'huda haNasi)

150 ~date for the **Apocryphic Gospels of the New Testament**

~date for earliest surviving *Sanskrit inscription (India)
~date for existing texts of the Shu Ching (**Chinese Classics,**
  see 2300 B.C.E.)
166 ~date for establishment of *Buddhism in China on a wider
  scale; earliest probable time for the Chinese
  Amitayurdhyana Sutra

late 2nd/early 3rd century

~date for the **Lotus Sutra** (*Buddhism)
~date for the **Mishnah** (Judaism)
~date for the teachings allegedly represented by the
  Sepher ha Zohar
~date for the **Buddha Charita** by Ashvagosha

3rd century

~beginning of the classical phase of Mayan civilization (ends
  c. 900) and the traditions of the **Pop Wuj**
~date for a canonized **Tao-te Ching**
200 ~date for the **Sepher ha Razim**
~date for the **Shata Shastra** by Aryadeva
~date for the **Huang-t'ing Ching**
~date for *Shenrab, the Buddha figure of Reformed *Bön
284–364 alchemist Ko Hung

4th century

~date for the **Guhyasamaja Tantra** and **Mahayana-
  samparigraha** by Asanga, founder of the *Yogacara
  school
~originating period of *Pahlavi **Denkart** (through the
  7th century)
~period for most of the **Puranas** (through the 13th century)
~date for the first compositions of **Midrash** text
  (through the 14th century)

17

300–400 ~date for the extant **Nag Hammadi Scriptures** in ★Coptic
300–500 actual collection of the **Tao-tsang** comes into existence
   320   ~date for the **Nei P'ing** by Ko Hung (see 220 B.C.E.)
   325   Council of Nicea; the Christian **Bible** in canonical form
   350   ~date for a written **Avesta** in the ★Pahlavi language
         ~date for the Jerusalem **Talmud** and the Gemara
365–408 dates for General Flavius Stilicho who willfully burned the
         Sibylline Books
   391   second destruction of the library at Alexandria, led by
         Christians

5th century

~earliest date for the Markandeya **Purana** and the
   Devi Mahatmya
~date for the **Abhidharmakosha** by Vasubandhu
~date for the Arya-Manjusri Mulakalpa and some early
   Samhitas, the Jayakhya Samhita, and Nisvasa-Tattva
   Samhita
~date for **Angas**, written in ★Prakrit (see 500 B.C.E.)
~date of first Chinese translation of the **Avatamsaka Sutra**
~date for Babylonian **Talmud** (through the 6th century)
400–450 codification of the Abhidharma (**Tripitaka**)
   404   completion of the Vulgate (Latin translation of the **Bible**)
   441   Council of Ephesus
470–543 ~dates for Bodhidharma, first patriarch of Ch'an ★**Buddhism**
         (China)

6th century

~date for the **Devi Purana** (★Shakta)
~date for the **Kubjika Tantra,** and perhaps for the
   Mahacinacara-sara Tantra
~beginning of oral formation of the **Eddas** (through the 7th
   century; see also 9th century and 1220)

18

538–552	~date for *Buddhism to reach Japan
550	last temple of the goddess Isis (at Philae) closed down (see **Hymns to Isis**)
550–606	Seng-ts'an (Jap., Sosan)
550–950	~date for the **Bundahishn**
570–632	the prophet Muhammad
595	~date for the **Hsin-hsin-ming** (China, Ch'an) by Seng-ts'an

7th century

possible origins of tales in the **Mabinogion** (Celtic Europe) (through the 9th century)

600–664	Hsüan-tsang (also San-tsang, or Sentsang), Chinese monk and translator/editor of the **San-tsang**
600–836	~time of "first diffusion of the doctrine" (Tibet, *Buddhism)
610	~date for the first texts of the **Qur'an** (Koran)
630	~date for the first **Hadith**
638–713	Hui-neng, or Wei-lang (Jap., E'no)
640	~date for a new, *Sanskrit-oriented Tibetan written language designed by Thon-mi sam-bho-ta
642	third destruction of the library at Alexandria, led by Muslims
644–656	~date for present, canonical form of the **Qur'an**
645–664	date for the **San-tsang** collection (China, *Buddhism)
late 7th	~date for the **Prajnopaya-viniscaya Siddhi** and the Samvara Tantra
	~date for the *Mahasiddha Ananga
	~date for the **Ginza** (Mandaean)

8th century

~date for the **T'an-ching** by Hui-neng (China, Ch'an)

~date for the **Hevajra Tantra** and **Kalachakra Tantra** and Jnanasiddhi Tantra

~date for Santideva and his Bodhicaryavatara (India, *Mahayana Buddhism)

~date for the formation of the **Teachings of the Golden Flower** (China, *Taoism)

~date for the Shodoka (China, Ch'an)

~date for the **Dharanis** (through the 9th century)

712   date for a written **Kojiki** (*Shinto)

717–804   ~dates for Padmasambhava

720   date for a written **Nihon Shoki,** or Nihongi (*Shinto)

742   canonization of the **Chuang-tzu** (China, *Taoism) (see 340 B.C.E.)

750–950   the various *Mahasiddhas develop and spread the teachings of Buddhist Tantra; oral formation of the first **Vajra Songs**

757–817   lifetime of Yeshe Tsogyal

760   ~date for the original **Bardo Thödol** (Tibet)

774–835   lifetime of Kobo Daishi, or Kukai (*Shingon)

780   ~date for the Sandokai (China, Ch'an)

~date for the *Mahasiddha Saraha

788–822   ~dates for Shankara (*Advaita Vedanta, India)

9th century

~time of the *Mahasiddhas Nagarjuna, Savaripa, Indrabhuti III, and Luipa (born c. 800); the Samvara Tantra reaches Tibet

~date for the Panchakrama, Amritesa Tantra, Kalottara Tantra, Kulacudamini Tantra, Kulasara Tantra, Mahakaulajnana Tantra, Malini-Vijayottara Tantra, Margendra Tantra, Paramesvaramata Tantra, Vamakesvara Tantra

~date for a written Poetic or Verse **Edda**

~date for the **Sepher Yetsirah**

~date for the Book of Johannes (Mandaean)

~date of canonization for many **Hadith**

~date for Shikand Gumani Vazar (Zoroastrianism)

806   **Kobo Daishi Zenshu** by Kukai

807–869   Ch'an master Tung-shan Liang-chieh

860 ~date for the **San-mei-k'o** (Jap., Hokyo Zanmai) by
      Tung-shan Liang-chieh
868 first printed book in China, the **Diamond Sutra**

10th century

~beginning of the "second diffusion of the doctrine"
    (Tibet, *Buddhism)
~date for the first texts of the Kagyu Gurtso (see **Vajra Songs**)
~date for the Devi Bhagavata (*Shakta)
~date for several of the **Yamalas**
~date for the **Abhidhammattha-sangaha** by Anuruddha
~date for the **Bundahishn** (Zoroastrianism)
~date for Bhutasuddhi Tantra, Chandamaharoshana Tantra,
    Dakini-Jala-Sambara Tantra, Heruka Tantra, Prapancara
    Tantra, Sadhanamala, Srikalachakra Tantra
900–1100 period of flowering for the *Shaiva tradition of *Hinduism,
      probable date for many of the **Agamas**
900–1300 possible time for the **Ganeshgita**
900–1500 period for the various extant Mesoamerican codices
      (see **Tonalpohualli**)
927 first edition of the **Engisiki** (*Shinto)
946 start of the Tibetan calendar; after arrival of the **Kalachakra**
      Tantra in Tibet
980–1052 Hsueh-tou Ch'ung-hsien (Japan, Setcho Juken), compiler of
      the **Pi Yän Lu** (Ch'an)
984–1082 Chang Po-tuan, founder of Complete Reality School of
      *Taoism
988–1069 the *Mahasiddha Tilopa

11th century

~date for the **Nila Tantra** and Paranada Sutra
~date for the Nispanna-Yogavalinama, Laksmi Tantra,
    Sarada Tilaka, and several of the **Yamalas**

~date for the Brahmanda **Purana** and the **Lalita Sahasranama**
1004   the **Ching-te ch'uan-teng-lu** of Tao-hsüan (Ch'an)
1016–1100   Naropa and his **Naro Chos-drug**
1039–1123   Milarepa
1040–1094   Javanese **Ramayana** by Yogisvara (Indonesia)
1052   the Brahma **Yamala**
1054   so-called Great Schism between the Christian Eastern and
        Western Churches
1063–1135   Yuan Wu (Japan, Bukka Engo), commentator on the
        Pi Yän Lu
1079–1153   Gampopa (see **Jewel Ornament of Liberation**)

12th century

~date for the **Mila Gnubum** (The Hundred Thousand
        Songs of Milarepa)
~date for the **Kularnava Tantra, Kaulavali Nirnaya Tantra,**
        and **Niruttara Tantra**
~date for the **Jewel Ornament of Liberation** by Gampopa
~date for written **Vajra Songs** of the *Mahasiddhas
~date for the Jayadratha **Yamala,** Matsyasukta Tantra, and
        Mahabhagavata **Purana** (*Shakta)
1115   ~date for the **Pi Yän Lu** (Ch'an)
1124   birth of Sun Bu-er
1130–1200   Chu Hsi, editor of the **Confucian Canon**
1133–1212   Honen (Japan, Pure Land)
1141–1215   Eisai, founder of the Rinzai school (Japan, *Zen)
1150   ~date for Kuo-an Shih-yuan (Jap., Kakuan Shien) and his
        Ten Pictures of the Ox (China)
        ~date for the Taoist **Li-chiao shih wu-lun**
1173–1262   Shonen Shinran (see **Tannisho**), a disciple of Honen (Japan)
1174   date for the Pingalamata
1175   ~date for the Sun Bu-er's Secret Texts (China, *Taoism)
1175–1200   ~date for compilation of **Confucianist Canon** by Chu Hsi
1179–1241   Snorri Sturluson (see **Edda**)

1183–1260	Wu-men Hui-k'ai (Jap., Mumon Enkai), compiler of the **Wu-men-kuan**
1190	~date for a first complete edition of the **Tao-tsang**
1191	foundation of *koan*-oriented Rinzai school by Eisai (Japan, *Zen)
late 12th	the **Mila Khabum** by the "Mad Yogi from gTsan"

13th century

~date for the **Codex Dresden** (see **Tonalpohualli**)

~date for the Parasurama-kalpa Sutra, the Barhaspatya Tantra, Bhuvanesvari Tantra, Chandrakala Tantra, Durvasasa Tantra, Jytisvari Tantra, Kalanidhi Tantra, Kulesvari Tantra, Bhagavata **Purana**

1200–1253	Dogen Kigen, or Dogen Eihei (see 1236 and **Shobo-genzo**)
1220	the Prose **Edda** by Snorri Sturluson
1222–1282	Japanese Buddhist reformer Nichiren
1236	foundation of Soto school by Dogen (Japan, *Zen)
1240–1305	Moses ben Shem Tov de Leon
1250	~date for the **Wu-men-kuan** (Ch'an), the **Shobo-genzo** (*Zen), and the **Tannisho** (Pure Land)
1270–1300	composition of the **Sepher ha Zohar** (see 200 C.E.)
1281	Mongol emperor Kublai Khan orders burning of the Tao-tsang
1290–1364	Bu-ston, compiler of the **Kanjur**

14th century

~date for the **Kanjur**/Tenjur (Tibet)

~date for the extended **Bardo Thödol**

~date for many of the **Yoga Upanishads**

~date for the Book of Balance and Harmony (see **I Ching**)

1300–1325	~dates for the writing of the White Book of Rhydderch (see **Mabinogion**)

1300–1500   period of final development of Mayan and Aztec
         hieroglyphic writing
     1323   Urgyan Lingpa (O-rgyan-gling-pa), *terton* of the **Life and**
         Liberation of Padmasambhava
     1368   Marco Polo in China
1375–1425   ~dates for the author of the Red Book of Hergest
         (see **Mabinogion**)

15th century

~date for the **Kalika Purana** (*Shakta)
~date for many other **Yoga Upanishads** (see 14th century)
~date for the Saktisamgama Tantra, Visvasara Tantra
1440–1518   ~dates for Kabir (Indian mystic and poet)
     1436   publication of extant, reduced edition of the **Tao-tsang**
1455–1570   Drugpa Künleg
     1456   first printed **Bible** (by Johannes Gutenberg, 1397–1468)
     1463   first Latin translation of the **Corpus Hermeticum**, first
         printing in 1471
1469–1538   Guru Nanak (India, Sikh)

16th century

~date for the **Yogini Tantra** and **Yoni Tantra**
~date for the Satcakra Nitupana
1522   **New Testament** translated into German (by Martin Luther,
     1483–1546)
1525   **New Testament** translated into English (by William
     Tyndale, 1494–1536)
1534   first complete **Bible** in German (by Martin Luther)
1535   first complete **Bible** in English (by Miles Coverdale,
     1488–1569), including the **Apocrypha** of the
     Old Testament

1539 ~date of birth for Arjan, the fifth guru (Sikh)
1546 Old Testamentarian **Apocrypha** accepted into the Biblical
      Canon by the Catholic church
1554–1558 ~date for a Popol Vuh written in the Spanish alphabet
      (see **Pop Wuj**)
1589 Mantra-Mahodadhi

17th century

printed version of the **Teachings of the Golden Flower**
      (China, ★Taoism)
1603/1604 ~date for first compilation of the **Adi Granth** by Arjan (Sikh)
1625–1710 Shiban Mangen and his Empo Dento-roku (Japan, ★Zen)
1629 the **Apocrypha** of the **Old Testament** are once more omitted
      from the Catholic **Bible**
mid 17th ~date for written Janam Sakhis (Sikh)
1680 ~date for the Tarabhakti-Sudharnava
late 17th ~date for third (and last) edition of the **Adi Granth** (Sikh)
      ~date for the **Gheranda Samhita** and **Shiva Samhita** (India,
      Yoga)

18th century

~date for the **Mahanirvana Tantra**
--date for the **Secret Life and Songs of the Lady Yeshe
      Tsogyal** (★Dzogchen and ★Nyingma-pa text)
1708 death of the tenth (and last) Sikh guru (see **Adi Granth**)
1750 ~date for the original **Walam Olum** (Delaware Indians)

19th century

1802–1884 Elias Lönnrot (see **Kalevala**)
1812 date for the Tantrasara

1812–1820 English translation of the **Walam Olum**
1817–1892 Baha'u'llah, or Mirza Husayn-'Ali (see **Kitab-i-Iqan**)
1819–1850 the Bab, or **Mirza 'Ali-Muhammad** (*Baha'i)
   1823 revelation of the **Book of Mormon** to Joseph Smith
        (1805–1844)
1835–1849 the Finnish **Kalevala** by Elias Lönnrot

20th century

   1926 first modern reproduction of the **Tao-tsang**
   1945 discovery of the **Nag Hammadi Scriptures**
1947–1956 discovery of the **Dead Sea Scrolls** from Qumran
   1973 discovery of oldest extant manuscripts of the **I Ching** and
        Tao-te Ching at Ma-wang-tui in central China
   1980 date for a **Pop Wuj** written in a Quiche alphabet
   1992 complete microfiche publication of the **Dead Sea Scrolls**

The
Divine
Library

First Shelf
5000 B.C.E.-500 B.C.E.

I Ching
Pyramid Texts
The Cycle of Inanna
Gilgamesh Epos
Coffin Texts
Enuma Elish
The Book of the Ever Deathless
Vedas
Rig Veda
Sama Veda
Yajur Veda
Gathas
Avesta
Iliad and Odyssey
Old Testament

---◆---

Atharva Veda
Genesis
Song of Songs (or Song of Solomon)
Aranyakas
Brahmanas
Upanishads
Yoga Sutra
Brihad-Aranyaka Upanishad
Tsalagi Teachings
Chandogya Upanishad
Mandukya Upanishad
Aitareya Upanishad
Sibylline Books
Tao-te Ching
Mahavamsa

I Ching

♦

This Book of Changes, also known as Yi King, is not only the oldest, but also the best known and most widely read of the five extant **Chinese Classics**. Reaching back in time for three to seven thousand years, it may well be the scripture containing the most ancient oral traditions still known to us. This ancient book of wisdom, alchemy, and self-analysis—which has been in written form for more than three thousand years—has been developed since the early phases of Chinese culture and has had several authors and none.

The earliest name associated with the I Ching (actually, with an even older form of divination, carried through time orally) is the prehistoric chieftain or emperor Fu Hsi, said to have lived in the years 2953–2838 B.C.E.—several I Ching specialists believe he may in fact have lived much earlier, perhaps as far back as 5000 B.C.E.

At a later stage, it was King Wen (b. 1191 B.C.E.) and his son, the Duke of Chou (c. 1160 B.C.E.), who made their impact on the developing texts. Another one thousand years later, by the second century B.C.E., Confucianist writers added their own views and insights to this work that was essentially of a rather Taoist orientation. Because many of the commentaries and appendices to the original text, the so-called wings, have sometimes been falsely attributed to K'ung-tzu (551–479 B.C.E.), the I Ching is sometimes regarded as part of the **Confucian Canon**, although there no evidence at all for his authorship.

The philosophical and divinatory basis of the I Ching is found in the permutations of the forces of yin (female, earth) and yang (male, heaven). The continuous interaction of these two basic and universal forces produces change (Chin., *I*), which is seen as the movement of the *Tao. The two dualistic yet complementary forces develop into the eight trigrams (three lines of yin or yang), which in turn combine into the sixty-four hexagrams (two trigrams and thus six lines). Some of the I Ching's symbolism also plays an important role in Taoist inner alchemy and subtle physiology (see *fang-chung shu*). The commentaries include, for example, the following statement: "The constant intermingling of Heaven and Earth

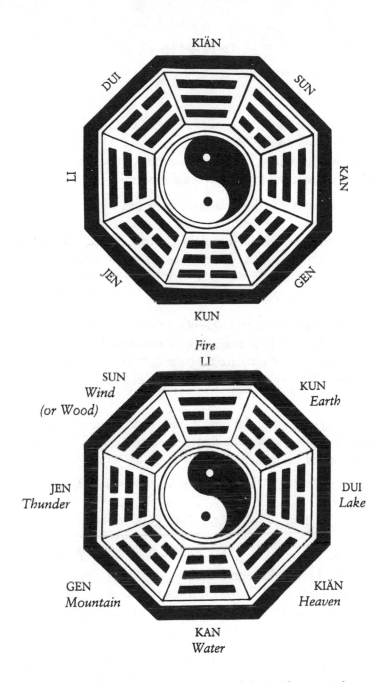

I Ching. Two traditional arrangements of the I Ching's eight trigrams. The upper hexagon, the system of Fu Hsi, differs from that of King Wen by presenting the trigrams in pairs of opposites.

gives shape to all things. The sexual union of man and woman gives life to all things." (van Gulik, 1974, p. 37).

In a fourteenth-century Taoist text, the Book of Balance and Harmony, the I Ching is discussed in the following words:

> If one does not read the Changes of sages, one will not understand the Changes of Heaven; if one does not understand the Changes of Heaven, one will not know the Changes of mind; if one does not know the Changes of mind, one will not be sufficiently able to master change. So we know that the Book of Changes is a book on the mastery of change. **(Cleary, 1986, p. 8)**

It will be interesting to see what new light is shed on this ancient text after the so-called Ma-wang-tui manuscripts, discovered in 1973, have been translated. This find, dating from about 200 B.C.E., includes a complete I Ching, the oldest extant manuscript.

Literature

There are very many translations of the I Ching and commentaries concerning it, and more are published almost annually. The following is a small selection of valuable and readily available texts only.

Blofeld, John, trans. *I Ching: The Book of Change*. London: Allen & Unwin, 1965.

Cleary, Thomas, trans. *The Taoist I Ching*. London and Boston: Shambhala, 1986.

Legge, James, trans. *I Ching: Book of Changes*. New York and London: Bantam Books, 1964. Reprint 1986.

Wilhelm, Richard. *The I Ching; or, Book of Changes*. Translated by Cary F. Baynes. Princeton, N.J.: Princeton University Press, 1967.

Pyramid Texts

♦

The most ancient of all preserved and translated religious documents of Egypt, by virtue of being cut into the stone walls of pyramids during the fifth and sixth dynasties (2494–2181 B.C.E.), are now referred to as the

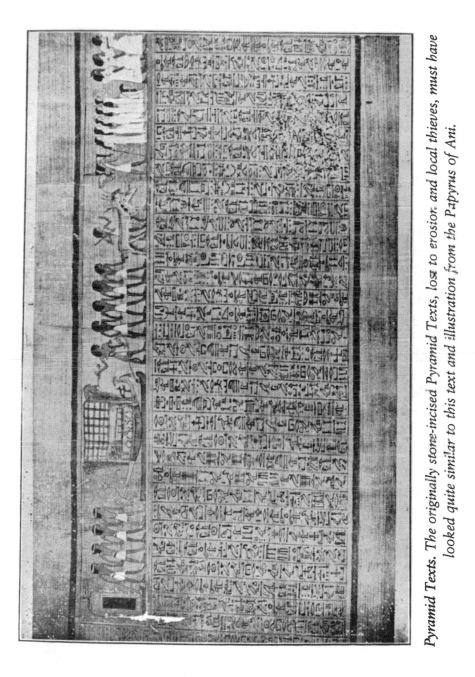

Pyramid Texts. The originally stone-incised Pyramid Texts, lost to erosion and local thieves, must have looked quite similar to this text and illustration from the Papyrus of Ani.

Pyramid Texts. The earliest-known of such texts were found in the pyramid of Unas, the last ruler of the fifth dynasty (c. 2300 B.C.E.), but similar texts also occur in the pyramids erected for his successors during the sixth dynasty. The concepts contained and presented in these writings, however, almost certainly originated at an even earlier, predynastic time (before 3100 B.C.E.), which places the oral traditions in the fifth and fourth millennia B.C.E. Many of the texts are concerned with matters of death and the associated royal funeral rites to ensure a rebirth and an immortal life together with the gods. As a result, these inscriptions have become known mainly as "funeral texts." Like other sacred texts, however, they are also concerned with the transmission of power from the realm of the divine to that of humans—reflecting the ultimate justification of rulership for the royal family, "divine ordination." The texts state that the king "is the son of the great wild-cow. She conceives him and gives birth to him" (Pyramid Text 1370), referring to the goddess Nuit, or Nut, in her form of the Great Cow. Earlier in the text, in a cosmological speculation on day and night, life and death, the same goddess is introduced in her aspect of Heavenly Mother and Star Goddess: "The star [sun] travels through the ocean beneath the body of Nut" (Pyramid Text 802).

Not much later, the tradition of the Pyramid Texts led to the development of the so-called **Coffin Texts** and the **Book of the Ever Deathless.** All these texts influenced Egyptian religion deeply and kept ancient beliefs alive; a particular example is the revival of interest in the ancient tradition during the twenty-sixth dynasty (664–525 B.C.E.). The renowned Egyptian Hymns to the Sun God are also based on the Pyramid Texts.

Literature
Faulkner, R. O. *The Ancient Egyptian Pyramid Texts.* Oxford: Clarendon Press, 1969.

The Cycle of Inanna
♦

Left to us in the form of fragmented tablets, in cuneiform writing, the story cycle concerning the Sumerian goddess Inanna (the Semitic Ishtar) is one of the oldest, and one of the most beautiful, epic poems of humanity. The poem, and the myths it recounts, include Sumerian and Akkadian elements of religious beliefs of the time.

Much of the material that constitutes this cycle was inscribed on clay tablets around 1750 B.C.E., but the conceptual content of the texts dates back to the beginning of the third millennium B.C.E. The work, which includes the famous story of the goddess's descent into the netherworld, provides us with ample testimony to the early religion(s) in which the goddess (the female, life and love) was at the heart of religion. At the same time, it surely is one of the earliest love poems ever recorded, and it is also one of the few myths that provide a truly positive role model for a woman's discovery of her self and her strength.

In the myths of Inanna, we also make acquaintance with the hero of the **Gilgamesh Epos**, another poem—part myth and part history—that affords insights into the very "cradle of civilization."

Literature

Wolkstein, Diane, and Samual Noah Kramer. *Inanna, Queen of Heaven and Earth: Her Stories and Hymns from Sumer.* New York: Harper & Row, 1983.

Gilgamesh Epos

♦

This Babylonian epic poem dated to about 1760 B.C.E. in its written form, found on clay tablets of the time, nonetheless includes much earlier material that goes back to the third millennium B.C.E. It is especially known for its description of the Babylonian version of the deluge, the Great Flood.

The poem tells the story of Gilgamesh, an archetypical "wanderer" who may be compared to the Greek Odysseus. Gilgamesh, said to be a son of the goddess Ninsun and of a high priest, is probably the first tragic character known to the literature of humanity; he is constantly being torn between the two aspects of himself: that of being godlike and that of being human. The story line begins with the hero's childhood and follows him through many

*Gilgamesh Epos. A fragment of the original clay tablets that
constitute the Gilgamesh Epos.*

adventures, until finally Gilgamesh's aim in life becomes to search for
wisdom and to gain immortality.

Unfortunately, the only English translation does not include a twelfth
tablet, thought by the editors to be incompatible with the rest of the story.
To date, a rendering of this part of the epic is only available in the French
edition and in an unpublished paper in Dutch by G. Meuleman.

Literature
Martin, Didier. *Un sage universel: L'épopée de Gilgamesh.* Paris: Editions
Garnier, 1979.

Gilgamesh Epos. A handwritten copy (by R. Campbell Thompson) of Tablet VII, iii, 33–48 clearly showing the cuneiform alphabet of the times.

Meuleman, G. *Het twaalfde tablet van het epos van Gilgamesh*. Unpublished manuscript. Amsterdam, 1990.

Sandars, N. K. *The Epic of Gilgamesh: An English Version with an Introduction*. Harmondsworth, England: Penguin Books, 1979.

Coffin Texts

♦

These texts constitute a development of the earlier **Pyramid Texts**, but they also represent a change in the attitudes and social circumstances of Egyptian civilization. Godlike immortality, or at least a pleasant type of afterlife, was now thought to be available not only to the royal family but to others as well. This applied to anyone able to afford a coffin inscribed with the appropriate prayers, spells, magical formulas, and praise of the divine powers. The inscriptions thus called Coffin Texts were most common during the eleventh (2133–1991 B.C.E.) and twelfth (1991–1786 B.C.E.) dynasties. The texts—insofar as they have been translated—allow us a

Enuma Elish. *An illustrated cuneiform tablet showing the Babylonian
sun god Shamash, the god of justice and even more exalted than
Marduk of the Enuma Elish. The name* shamash *has been
preserved in Hebrew, where it is the term for sun.*

glance at Egyptian mythology and religious concepts from around 2000 B.C.E. About four hundred years later, this custom was superseded by a new development, as can be gleaned from the Egyptian **Book of the Ever Deathless.**

Literature
Faulkner, R. O. *The Ancient Egyptian Coffin Texts*. 3 vols. Warminster: Aris & Phillips, 1973–1977.

Enuma Elish
♦

The title of this epic poem represents the epic's first two words, meaning "when on high." It is the Akkadian—that is, Babylonian and Assyrian—epic of creation, comparable to Genesis and other early cosmological speculations on the beginning of the universe and the world.

The text, contained in seven clay tablets, is heavily dependent on influences from Sumerian culture and recounts the mythical struggle between the god Marduk and the primal ocean, in the form of the goddess Tiamat, a struggle that resulted in the creation of heaven and earth. Humanity is created, according to this legend, from the blood of a rebel god, in order to free all deities from menial labor. The ancient myth was reenacted annually during the so-called enthronement festival, a Babylonian New Year, in which the current king played the role of Marduk.

The Book of the Ever Deathless
♦

A later development of the **Pyramid** and **Coffin Texts,** the various chants and magical spells of this text collection were designed to assist the departing soul in facing judgment, at which each person's soul was thought to be weighed and judged by the gods Anubis, Thoth, and Osiris.

The title's usual translation, the Book of the Dead, is one of those misnomers rooted in misunderstanding or in religious chauvinism. More

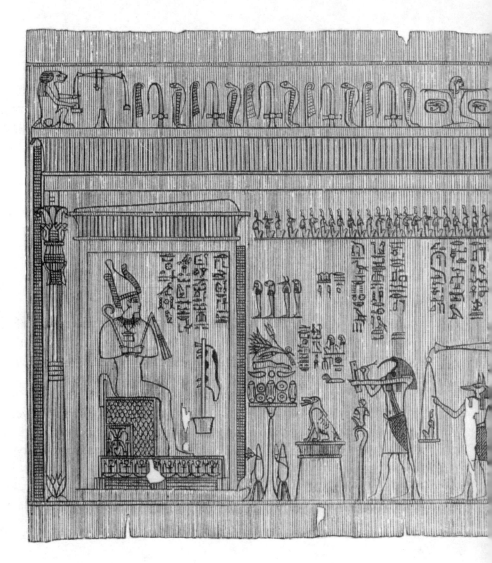

true to the Egyptian title, which translates as "Coming Forth by Day," is the English rendering as "The Book of the Ever Deathless," which communicates a rather different idea: that of a rebirth or, at least, a continuation of life after death. The texts, full of magical spells and accompanying the deceased in the tomb, allowed her or him to go forth from the tomb at will.

The Book of the Ever Deathless is a collection of texts that have been

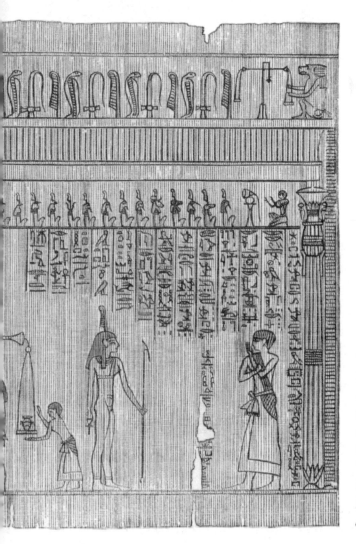

The Book of the Ever Deathless. The soul of a recently deceased is weighed on the scale and the judgment is recorded by the god Thoth (immediately left of the scale), the inventor of writing and divine scribe.

found in various tombs, with the individual papyri showing a variety of contents. Taken as a whole, they enable us to get a reasonably clear image of Egyptian values and of their religious beliefs about both life and life after death. The various "Coming Forth" texts underwent major revisions during the Saite period, the twenty-sixth dynasty (664–525 B.C.E.), when parts were deleted and others were rewritten or added on; this version is now known as the Saite rescension.

Literature

Allen, T. G., trans. *The Book of the Dead; or, Going Forth By Day.* Chicago: University of Chicago Press, 1974.

Budge, E. A. Wallis. *The Book of the Dead.* 2nd ed., rev. and enlarged. London: Kegan Paul, Trench, Trubner & Co., 1928. London: Arkana, 1989.

Vedas

♦

Composed in an archaic form of *Sanskrit known as Vedic, the Vedas (Skt., "wisdom," "knowledge") are India's most ancient collection of sacred scriptures. These texts consist of hymns, legends, and treatises on ritual, magic, cosmology, and medicine. Though dating the texts has proved to be very difficult, the Vedas are generally thought to have been transmitted orally beginning around 1550 B.C.E., with the exception perhaps of the **Atharva Veda**. In a written form, however, none of the works were codified until 600 B.C.E., and the Atharva Veda was not codified until as late as 200 B.C.E.

The general and collective name applies to four (sometimes only three) major divisions of these ancient documents, individually known as **Rig Veda, Sama Veda, Yajur Veda,** and **Atharva Veda**. The Vedic hymns are traditionally regarded as revelations (Skt., *shruti*), as having been "seen" or "received" by the ancient sages during specific, higher states of consciousness. There are indications that each of the first three Vedic collections were prepared for different classes of Brahmin priests, each of whom had different functions during the sacrifices. In another sense, and after centuries of literary development, each individual Veda consists of four different classes of texts:

1. **Samhitas,** the most ancient collections of Vedic hymns.
2. **Brahmanas,** texts mainly concerning rituals.
3. **Aranyakas,** specific interpretations for those undergoing forest retreats.
4. **Upanishads,** the "end of the Vedas," mystical or psychological

Vedas. An early nineteenth-century representation of a typical rishi *(Skt.,* rsi)*, a Vedic seer. Bengali woodcarving.*

interpretations, commentaries, and teachings often departing from the ancient teachings themselves.

A problem with these four terms lies in the fact that they have also been used, at later times, for other types of sacred scriptures, often in an attempt to have those texts gain a certain authority.

See also **Mahabharata.**

Literature

Müller, Max, trans. *Vedic Hymns.* Sacred Books of the East series, Max Müller, ed., vols. 32, 46. Oxford: Clarendon Press, 1884. Reprint. Delhi: Motilal Banarsidass, 1967.

Rig Veda

◆

The Rig Veda's collection of 1,028 hymns was transmitted orally beginning about 1550 B.C.E., whereas a written edition in Vedic *Sanskrit appeared only after 600 B.C.E. In ten chapters, this most ancient part of the **Vedas** contains rules and regulations concerning sacrifices, public and domestic ceremonies, and the religious, cosmological speculations of the invading Aryan peoples of this early age. The Rig Veda (Skt., "hymnic knowledge") is also very much concerned with the preparation and use of *soma and seems to have been the special collection for use by those Brahmins whose task it was to call or invoke the gods.

The texts also feature a number of essentially chauvinist opinions held by the then-invading Aryan peoples with regard to the Dravidian inhabitants of India, doctrines that are at the root of India's rigid caste system. Although the Rig Veda is mainly patriarchal, with most hymns dedicated to one or another of the Aryan gods, the text does already mention *Shakti, the major goddess of the later traditions of *Tantra and *Shakta. Also the term *yoga* is used often in these texts, in its general sense of "discipline" and not as referring to Yoga as we now know it. A number of hymns from this text also appear in the **Atharva Veda.**

Literature

Arnold, E. V. *The Rig Veda.* New York: AMS Press, 1972.

Griffith, Ralph T.H., trans. *The Hymns of the Rig Veda.* 4 vols. Delhi: Nag Publishers, 1973.

Wilson, H. H., trans. *Rig-Veda-samhita: A Collection of Ancient Hindu Hymns.* 2nd ed. London: N. Trubner, 1866– .

Sama Veda

♦

Part of the **Vedas,** this is a collection of hymns and songs to be recited during the preparation and commencement of the *soma sacrifice. The text differs only slightly from the **Rig Veda,** featuring a specific selection from that source for the purpose of chanting. The Sama Veda seems to have been the special collection for use by those Brahmins who actually performed the prescribed sacrifices.

Two **Upanishads** belonging to this Vedic collection are the Kena and Chandogya Upanishad.

For literature, see Vedas.

Yajur Veda

♦

Subdivided into Black Yajus and White Yajus, this part of the **Vedas** constitutes a prose manual intended as instruction and guide for the priests performing the prescribed sacrifices. Simultaneously, the Yajur Veda (Skt., "sacrifice knowledge") seems to have been the special collection for use by those Brahmins who were known as the "chanters" (Skt., *udgatri*) and who had to intone the appropriate hymns before and during the sacrificial rituals.

Upanishads belonging to the White collection are the Isha and **Brihad-Aranyaka Upanishad,** whereas the Katha and Taittiriya Upanishad belong to the Black Yajur Veda.

See also **Brahmanas.**

For literature, see Vedas.

Gathas

♦

These chants of the prophet Zarathushtra (Zoroaster) are part of the Persian **Avesta,** but were written in what is called Gathic, a language that differs from the rest of that work. According to new findings they probably originated in the Persia of about 1500 B.C.E., though legend places them even earlier (5000 B.C.E.); conservative science dates them to only the seventh and sixth centuries B.C.E.

Only nineteen of these hymns have survived, the only texts by the prophet himself, and they constitute chapters 28–34, 41–51, and 53 of the Yasna (see **Avesta**). The major topic of early Persian religion, the eternal struggle between the forces of light and darkness, also plays a strong role in these Gathas, which seem to have been used as liturgical chants in order to dispel the evil spirits under the leadership of the dark god or demon Angra Mainyu.

Literature

Insler, S. *The Gathas of Zarathushtra.* Acta Iranica, third series, vol. 1. Leiden, Netherlands: Brill, 1975.

Avesta

♦

This is the collective name for the sacred scriptures of the Persian religion(s) inspired by Zarathushtra (sixth or sixteenth century B.C.E.; scientific opinions differ). Today, the Zoroastrian school of thought is partly continued

*Avesta. An ancient Babylonian cylinder seal showing the winged sun
and the sacred tree that are spoken of in the Avesta
and other Zoroastrian writings.*

by the Parsees, Persians who fled to India after the Arab/Islamic conquest
of their homeland in the eighth century C.E. The religion is most often
known as Zoroastrianism, though this is actually only one of more developments within the main framework set up by Zarathushtra.

Most of the book is written in an old Persian language known as Avestan,
one of the alphabets that developed from early *Aramaic. The oldest collection of texts, once destroyed by Alexander in 330 B.C.E. and rewritten by the
priests from memory, was finally codified in about 350 C.E. and comprises
four classes of writings:

1. Yasna (worship or adoration; yasna is also the term used to indicate
   Zoroastrian public worship): Mainly texts of a liturgical character
   written for the priests. Among these are several chapters known as
   the **Gathas** (chants), the actual writings of Zarathushtra, written in
   an early language that differs from the rest of the Avesta.

47

2. Yasht or Yast (sacrifice): This part of the Avesta mainly contains sacrificial hymns directed to various individual deities.
3. Vendidad (laws against demons): Mainly a collection of ritual and religious law, but also containing much mythological and legendary material. The text is usually read during a nightly office.
4. Zend or Zand: In later recordings of the Avesta, these are added secondary texts and learned commentaries to the original texts. The whole collection is therefore sometimes known as Zend-Avesta.

See also **Bundahishn.**

Texts of the early Avesta, with their hymns and prayers to such deities as Mithra, Indra, and Varuna, point to the common Indo-Iranian origin of these gods, who also achieved much fame in the India of the early **Vedas.**

Literature
Darmesteter, J. *The Zend-Avesta. Part 1: The Vendidad.* Delhi: Banarsidass, 1965.
———. *The Zend-Avesta. Part 2: The Sirozahs, Yashts, and Nyayesh.* Delhi: Banarsidass, 1965.
Mills, L. H. *The Zend-Avesta. Part 3: The Yasna, Visparad, Gahs, and Miscellaneous Fragments.* Delhi: Banarsidass, 1965.

Iliad and Odyssey

♦

These classical works of Greek mythology and traditional history are perfect examples of the transformation of oral traditions into written works. Although these epics were long thought to have been conceived by Homer (eighth century B.C.E.), it is now certain that the famous Greek only collected and poetically edited existing, older material. A living and dynamic oral tradition—ancient memories full of social, ethical, and judicial guidelines—thus became fixed. The almost magical fascination the books hold, even over peoples of much later ages, depends to a large degree upon

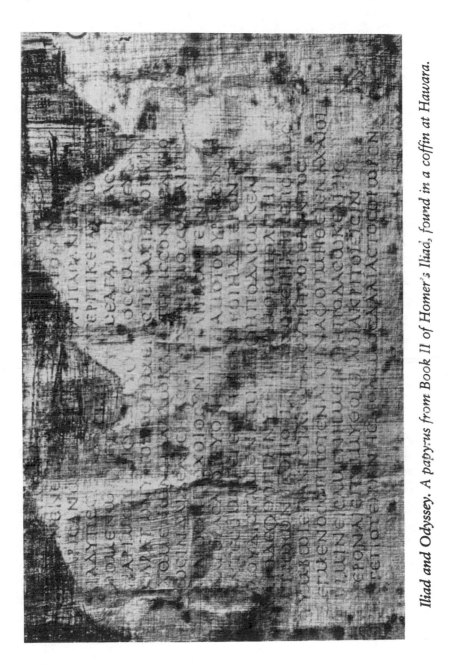

Iliad and Odyssey. A papyrus from Book II of Homer's Iliad, found in a coffin at Hawara.

the language and metaphors used by a preliterate people, a language meant to be recited and listened to.

The Iliad, consisting of twenty-eight books, reaches back in time to 1194 B.C.E. and is an epic concerned mainly with the fall of Troy. The voluminous text recounts the events during only fifty-one days of the last year of the Trojan War.

The Odyssey, on the other hand, recalls the ten years of Odysseus' adventurous travels and is, basically, a hymn celebrating his safe return home. Considering that Odysseus was also involved in the Trojan War, this epic seems also to go back in time to about 1200 B.C.E.

Literature

Beye, Charles R. *The Iliad, the Odyssey, and the Epic Tradition*. London: Macmillan, 1968.

Kirk, Geoffrey. *The Songs of Homer*. Cambridge: Cambridge University Press, 1962.

Old Testament

♦

This is the collective name for the thirty-nine older books of the Christian **Bible** and coinciding with what is often called the Hebrew Bible. The Old Testament is thus revered as sacred scripture in both Judaism and Christianity (and partly in Islam), and as a national, historical epos by the peoples of Israel.

The collection of books of the Old Testament must be understood as describing, in a rather archetypal manner, the historical and crucial transition of large groups of people from a tribal, nomadic lifestyle to that of settled farmers and citizens, with all the ramifications accompanying such drastic changes: social, political, and economic struggles between states and religions, peoples and individuals. On a symbolic level, this transition also reflects the (forced) departure from a general worship of the Near Eastern Great Goddess(es) and the ascension of a sole male creator and ruler, also resulting, in diverse ways, in a struggle between men and women.

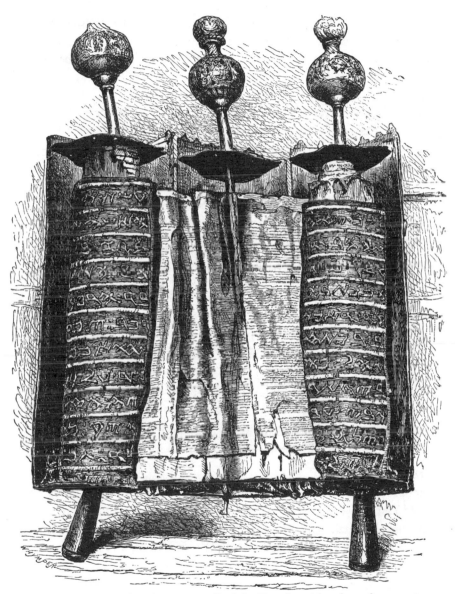

Old Testament. *A handwritten roll of the Torah, said to have been written by Eleazar, son of Aaron.*

The various texts, put into writing during the span of time between about 1000 B.C.E. and 164 B.C.E., are often based on and include historic and folkloric material that is much older. The originally Hebrew texts were first translated into Greek about 285 B.C.E., a collection known as the Septuagint.

Formally, the thirty-nine books of the Old Testament are often subdivided into the following three classes:

1. The Five Books of the Law of Moses: These are the texts that, according to tradition, were received by Moses on Mount Sinai. Known as the Torah in Judaism and as the Pentateuch in Christianity, these first five books (**Genesis**, Exodus, Leviticus, Numbers, and Deuteronomy) also form the basis for the much later, cabalistic **Sepher ha Zohar.**

2. The Prophetic Books: In these books of the prophets Joshua, Isaiah, and so forth, including the twelve minor prophets, God speaks to his potential believers, before they, in the next section, speak to God (in the Psalms). The language used by both types of texts is as often sacred as it is profane.

3. The Didactic Books: Also known as the Writings, this third division of the Old Testament comprises what is called "wisdom literature" (such as Job and Proverbs) and is sometimes also concerned with love (**Song of Songs**), speaking of the spiritual and physical realms of knowledge that are part of the experience of life. The Psalms belong here as well as the later histories and related material.

See also **Apocrypha and Pseudepigraphia of the Old Testament.**

Literature

Pritchard, James Bennett, ed. *Ancient Near Eastern Texts Relating to the Old Testament.* 3rd ed. Princeton, N.J.: Princeton University Press, 1969.

Sandmel, Samuel. *The Hebrew Scriptures: An Introduction to Their Literature and Religious Ideas.* New York: Knopf, 1963.

Atharva Veda

♦

This fourth Veda is the youngest of all the **Vedas** and was for a long time not even recognized as a true part of Vedic literature. Its preliterate roots seem to reach back to about 1000 B.C.E., yet a written collection appeared only in about 200 B.C.E. Its contents were not clearly fixed and delineated, and some of its parts were originally regarded as belonging to the **Yajur Veda**—a division of the texts which thus resulted in the Trayi, or Threefold, Veda.

The Atharva contains 731 hymns copied from the **Rig Veda,** yet it also includes some other texts—magical incantations and metaphysical speculations—that had once been judged too controversial or "uninspired," leading to their exclusion from the official Vedic canon. The fourth Veda deals mainly with medicinal concerns: the power of healing and associated rites and magical spells. It contains a number of references that hint at early precursors of deities, rites, and techniques that are part of later Yoga (breath control) and *Tantra; for example, Mahanagni and Mahavrata.

According to tradition, the original Atharva Veda had an appendix known as Ayur Veda (Skt., "life science"); the actual texts are no longer available, yet this term remains the name for India's traditional system of medicine, the wisdom of which has been preserved in other texts. Of the **Upanishads** that belong to this Veda, only the **Mandukya,** Mundaka, and Prashna Upanishads are recognized by traditional Vedantists.

Literature

Bloomfield, Maurice, trans. *Hymns of the Atharva-Veda, Together with Extracts from the Ritual Books and the Commentaries.* Sacred Books of the East series, Max Müller, ed., vol. 42. Oxford: Clarendon Press, 1897. Reprint. Delhi: Motilal Banarsidass, 1973.

Genesis

◆

Genesis is the first book of the Torah and thus of the **Old Testament,** and probably one of the most essential texts of both the Hebrew and the Christian **Bible;** most certainly to the cabalists of later ages. The text was apparently composed in postexilic times (after 538 B.C.E.) but includes, as is so often the case, oral traditions that reach back in time much further, certainly to at least 950 B.C.E.

The book consists of cosmological speculations similar to those of other cultures of the time and region. To a greater extent than its contemporary cosmologies, however, it proposed an unnameable, ineffable, and jealous divinity as sole creator of the universe and of humanity. Genesis contains, together with myths and legends clearly deriving from Babylonia and Egypt, the famous story of Eve's disobedience and her courageous rebellion against a law intended to keep humanity ignorant of the difference between good and evil. The text also recounts the submission of several cultures and religions to the patriarch Abraham (c. 2000–1900 B.C.E.) and his armies, the change from human sacrifice to that of animals, and it offers many allegorical stories intended to spread certain codes of behavior among the nomadic peoples of the times.

See also **Bible, Old Testament.**

Literature
Suares, Carlo. *The Cipher of Genesis: The Original Code of the Qabala As Applied to the Scriptures.* Boulder and London: Shambhala, 1978.

Song of Songs (or Song of Solomon)

◆

This is one of the books in the **Old Testament,** usually attributed to Solomon (990–922 B.C.E.), son of David (c. 1010–c. 962 B.C.E.) and king of Israel, famous for his wisdom and his intuitive judgments concerning human affairs. Although attributed to this sage-king, the work in its written form dates to not earlier than about 350 B.C.E., a time when it had been transmitted orally for at least six hundred years.

The "song" is a collection of inspired love poems that are regarded by many as allegorical only, speaking not of the love between men and women but rather of love between humans and the divine. Whereas many ortho-dox Jewish and Christian scholars and believers are confused or unhappy with the Song's inclusion in the canonical **Bible,** it is regarded as a very important text among cabalists and is one of the eighteen parts of the **Zohar.** Considering the cultural origins of the texts, they can easily be imagined to be meant literally, actually speaking of human love—which they do on an exoteric level. On the other hand, they represent an encoded cabalistic wisdom similar to that used in **Genesis** and in the **Sepher Yetsirah.**

Another name by which this text is known is Canticles. Other works attributed to Solomon, his odes and psalms, are part of the apocryphal Old Testamentarian literature.

See also **Bible, Old Testament.**

Literature
Suares, Carlo. *The Song of Songs.* Berkeley and London: Shambhala, 1972.

Aranyakas
♦

Intended as texts for use by forest-dwelling adepts and hermits, the Aranyakas (Skt., "pertaining to the woods") are more or less supplementary texts to the Vedic collections known **as Samhitas** and their respective **Brahmanas.** The works, each associated with a specific collection of the **Vedas,** represent the philosophical point of departure from which the Brahmanas begin, to be ultimately superseded by the **Upanishads.** They usually contain information about important ritual matters as well as mystical reflections designed to aid the solitary adept on his path. Considering that these texts usually preceded the classical Upanishads, which are generally dated to the eighth to fifth centuries B.C.E., one should, in the absence of clear data, date the Aranyakas to about 900 B.C.E. to 500 B.C.E.

In later collections of the texts, an Aranyaka can sometimes contain an

Upanishad, as for example the **Aitareya Upanishad** that is part of the Aitareya Aranyaka.

Literature
Keith, Arthur B., ed. and trans. *Sankhyana Aranyaka.* London: Royal Asiatic Society, 1908.
————. *Aitareya Aranyaka.* London: Royal Asiatic Society, 1909. Reprint 1969.

Brahmanas
♦

Brahmanas is a designation for a number of clerical compositions associated with the **Vedas,** or Vedic **Samhitas,** mainly explaining and expounding Vedic sacrificial rituals and their underlying symbolism. The oldest of the Brahmanas, the Shatapatha Brahmana of the **Yajur Veda,** has been dated to approximately 900 B.C.E., yet most of the works seem to have been written during the eighth to fifth centuries B.C.E.

It is mainly through these scriptures that the *Sanskrit term *brahman* acquired its meaning of "the Absolute" in the sense of a universal divine principle. Earlier, the term meant simply "to grow," "vast," and "expanse."(The term *brahman* for the highly abstract, philosophical concept of a highest principle should not be confused with the name Brahma, the god of creation in the classical all-male trinity of *Brahmanism and /or *Hinduism.)

The texts are closely interwoven with other Vedic literature such as the **Upanishads,** the latter of which often show strong influences from the mysticism prevalent in many of the Brahmanas.

Literature
Keith, Arthur B., trans. *Rigveda Brahmanas: Aitareya and Kausitaka Brahmanas of the Rigveda.* Harvard Oriental Series 25. Cambridge, Mass.: Harvard University Press, 1920. Reprint 1971.

Upanishads

♦

This term is often translated as "secret doctrine," although the actual *Sanskrit words speak of "sitting close to one's teacher"— listening to his inspired teachings and wisdom. The Upanishads are regarded as more or less authoritative summaries of the philosophy and moral codes of the Vedas and of traditional *Hinduism in general. Most of the works were written by anonymous Indian sages and scholars some time between 800 B.C.E. and 400 B.C.E. At a later time the texts came to be regarded as major scriptures in their own right and were considered to be inspired revelations (Skt., *shruti*). For this reason, these texts are also known as *Vedanta, a term that means "the end of the Vedas."

No general consensus exists as to the number of Upanishads. Traditionally, they are considered to number 108, but the actual number is simply unknown. Likewise no consensus exists as to which, and how many, texts are considered the "principal" Upanishads. Numbers range from ten to eighteen, and scholars and translators often seem to make personal choices in this regard. According to the eighth-century Indian philosopher Shankara, there are ten principal texts, and each can be classified as being associated with one of the four Vedas, as follows:

Yajur Veda: Isha, Katha, Taittiriya, and Brihad-Aranyaka Upanishads

Sama Veda: Kena and Chandogya Upanishads

Rig Veda: Aitareya Upanishad

Atharva Veda: Mundaka, Prashna, and Mandukya Upanishads

In general, these scriptures reflect the Vedas in the importance they attribute to the powers released through sacrifices. The Upanishads nonetheless differ from the older Vedas in that they focus much more on what goes on inside humans, on psychological processes and states of consciousness. The texts further develop the idea of *brahman,* the highest concept of a divine principle in *Brahmanism, and speculate extensively on how the individual soul (Skt., *atman*) can be united with *brahman* by methods of contemplation and meditation. They also dwell on the concept of karma—the effects of a person's actions in life—and on how to overcome this causality by means of renunciation and through spiritual exercises such as meditation.

Originally these works were intended to be transmitted to members of the upper three castes only, but today most of the texts are accessible to anyone who seeks to read them.

See also **Yoga Upanishads.**

Literature

Alyar, K. Narayanasvami. *Thirty Minor Upanishads.* El Reno, Okla.: Santarasa Publications, 1980.

Deussen, Paul. *Sixty Upanishads of the Veda.* 2 vols. Delhi: Motilal Banarsidass, 1990.

Easwaran, Eknath, trans. *The Upanishads.* London: Routledge & Kegan Paul, 1988.

Müller, Max, trans. *The Upanishads.* Sacred Books of the East series, Max Müller, ed., vols. 5, 15. Oxford: Clarendon Press, 1897. Reprint. Delhi: Motilal Banarsidass, 1965.

Radhakrishnan, Sarvepalli, trans. *The Principal Upanishads.* 4 vols. London: Allen & Unwin, 1953.

Yoga Sutra

♦

This work, consisting of 195 (sometimes 196) Yoga aphorisms arranged in four chapters, is regarded as the most authoritative text of the classical system of Yoga. This concise exposition of Yoga philosophy and practice, systematized by Patanjali, is based on an earlier tradition known among scholars as *preclassical yoga,* which most likely began about 800 B.C.E. Parts of this system can be found in other texts such as the **Bhagavadgita,** the **Mahabharata,** and several **Upanishads.**

Yoga Sutra. A contemporary illustration showing a yogi in meditation. Ancient practitioners were often seated on a tigerskin, one of their few material possessions. The drawing also shows the seven centers (chakras) *of the human subtle body.*

Patanjali was a student of Ashtavakra (second century B.C.E.), author of the important **Ashtavakra Samhita.** Patanjali departs in his teachings from the nondualism of *Vedanta and embraces a dualistic interpretation of reality and its phenomena. The work also shows influences from *Mahayana Buddhism, which, at the time, was developing and slowly gaining ground. Although dates for Patanjali, and thus for his text, are far from clearly established, most scholars place his period of teaching and writing at around 150 B.C.E.

The text itself is also known as Patanjala Sutra.

Literature

There are many translations of Patanjali's work and commentaries concerning it. The following is a small selection of texts only.

Feuerstein, Georg. *The Yoga Sutra of Patanjali: A New Translation and Commentary.* Rochester, Vt.: Inner Traditions, 1990.

Taimni, I. K., trans. *The Science of Yoga: The Yoga-Sutras of Patanjali.* Madras: Theosophical Publishing House, 1961.

Woods, James Haughton. *The Yoga-System of Patanjali.* Delhi: Motilal Banarsidass, 1966.

Brihad-Aranyaka Upanishad

♦

The "Secret Teachings from the Great Forest" is probably the oldest of the Upanishads, with parts of it dating back to the eighth century B.C.E. This longest of all Upanishads, an almost encyclopedic work with many references to, and quotes from, the Vedas, is known not only for its profound discussion of the concept of the self, but also for the attention paid to the text in the form of a unique commentary by the renowned monist philosopher Shankara (788–822 C.E.). Further, it is of special interest in that its writer/composer paid much attention to the then-arising doctrines concerning the possible liberation from the otherwise endless wheel of rebirth or reincarnation. The Brihad-Aranyaka Upanishad is, in fact, a text found within the Shatapatha Brahmana, part of the Yajur Veda and probably the best known among the Brahmanas.

For literature, see Upanishads.

Tsalagi Teachings

♦

For almost three thousand years, the teachings collected under this title apparently have been transmitted purely orally, until a member of the Cherokee tribe, Dhyani Ywahoo, recently published parts of this tradition in a work entitled *Voices of Our Ancestors.* Her book presents a number of traditional "teaching stories" of the Tsalagi, the "principal people" known in English as the Cherokee tribe. The function of such stories is to transmit the tribe's views concerning the individual, social, and cosmic realities and their interplay. The topics of these teaching stories range from origin stories, such as the legendary descent of the "principle people"from the stars to the earth, to stories and allegories clearly designed to teach social psychology to those listening when sitting around the fire. In the author's own words, "the basis of these teachings is to infuse each moment [of life] with the three fundamental principles of intention, compassion and doing good." Dhyani Ywahoo is a member of the Cherokee's Ywahoo, a lineage of individuals that can be compared to the Celtic bards, whose office and duty it was to transmit teachings from generation to generation; the author describes this lineage in her tribe as reaching back 2,860 years.

Literature
Ywahoo, Dhyani. *Voices of Our Ancestors: Cherokee Teachings from the Wisdom Fire.* Boston: Shambhala, 1987.

Chandogya Upanishad

♦

This is perhaps second oldest of the Upanishads; it is associated with the Sama Veda collection and was composed sometime during the seventh or eighth century B.C.E. It represents the secret teaching (Skt., *upanishad*) of the Chandogya school. In eight chapters, the work presents the fundamental teachings of early Vedic *Hinduism concerning cosmology, the individual and universal soul, and afterlife. The Chandogya is best known for its elaborate discussion of the early concept of the life force (Skt., *prana*) and for its lengthy and detailed speculations on the sacred syllable *om*. The text also contains the often-quoted Vedic saying *Tat tvam asi,* or "That thou art."

For literature, see Upanishads.

Mandukya Upanishad

◆

This is a very short work that belongs to the **Atharva Veda** collection. The text is especially interesting in that it testifies to the fact that oral repetition, not reading, was the intended mode of use. The Mandukya is clearly a chant or prayer with great mnemonic value, focusing especially on the sacred syllable *om*. The eighth-century scholar and philosopher Shankara declared this to be the one **Upanishad** to be studied in case one cannot afford to do more.

For literature, see Upanishads.

Aitareya Upanishad

◆

This **Upanishad** is part of the **Rig Veda** collection and is contained in the Aitareya **Aranyaka**. The twenty-five-hundred-year-old text is a unique creation story that especially makes interesting reading when compared to other accounts of creation such as the Akkadian **Enuma Elish** or the biblical **Genesis**. Composed in simple, down-to-earth language, the Aitareya Upanishad takes a very "modern," almost quantum-dynamic, approach to reality and to the mind's participation in creating and shaping it.

For literature, see Upanishads.

Sibylline Books

♦

A term used for the Etruscan/Roman oracular books written by, or attributed to, a number of prophetic women known as sibyls, who lived and practiced throughout the Mediterranean and Near Eastern area. Most famous among these was the sibyl of Cumae, near Naples, and most of the Roman books, nine in number, have been attributed to her. The Sibylline Books were bought from the sibyl Cumae by an Etruscan ruler in the sixth century B.C.E., testifying to an even earlier existence of the texts. Some of these works perished in a fire in 83 B.C.E., the others were burned by order of the Roman general Flavius Stilicho (365–408 C.E.), after the books had been consulted for the last time.

Several of the works, influencing Jewish writings of the time and being influenced in turn, have a truly prophetic character; others mainly contained spells and prescriptions designed to aid in overcoming bad fortune and disaster. Often, the sibyls and their books were instrumental in advocating the inclusion of imported religious beliefs, rituals, and deities—mainly of Greek origin—into mainstream religious practice of the Roman empire.

The works were jealously guarded, in the temple of Jupiter, by an exclusive college of priests who consulted the books on request by the Roman senate. The texts are not extant, but several well-known historians and authors of the times did copy some parts of the works or at least reported on the books.

Parts of this tradition are reflected in the pseudepigraphic Sibylline Oracles (see **Apocrypha and Pseudepigraphia of the Old Testament**).

Literature

Spenser, Terry Milton, trans. *Oracula Sibyllina*. New York: Cranston & Stowe, 1890.

老子
道可道非常道名可名非常名無名天地之始
有名萬物之母常無欲以觀其妙常有欲以觀
其徼此兩者同出而異名同謂之玄玄之又玄眾
妙之門
天下皆知美之為美斯惡已皆知善之為善斯不
善已故有無之相生難易之相成長短之相形高
下之相傾音聲之相和前後之相随是以聖人處

Tao-te-Ching. Text fragment from a fourteenth-century Tao-te Ching, inscribed in stone by Chao Meng-fu in 1316.

64

Tao-te Ching

♦

In this most famous of Taoist texts, its alleged author Lao-tzu (c. 580–500 B.C.E.) uses the term *Tao in a metaphysical sense—as that of an all-embracing first principle and primordial source of all things—for the first time. In the terms of contemporary scientists, this comes close to what David Bohm calls the "enfolded reality" from which all unfoldment has yet to proceed. Rather than using such intellectual constructs, the Tao-te Ching prefers to teach:

> *The ways that can be walked are not the eternal Way;*
> *The names that can be named are not the eternal name.*
> *The nameless is the origin of the myriad creatures;*
> *The named is the mother of the myriad creatures.*
>
> (H. V. Mair, trans., verse 45 [previously verse 1])

Several contemporary scholars and scientists consider the authorship of Lao-tzu, or even his existence at all, to be rather uncertain. The Tao-te Ching may have had several authors or perhaps none: the text is rooted in an oral tradition (c. 650–350 B.C.E.) that was finally put into writing around the third century B.C.E.

The discovery in 1973 of previously unknown manuscripts at the site of Ma-wang-tui has made available a text that is almost five hundred years older than previously extant versions. New translations are now becoming available that add to our understanding of the text and can rectify previous incorrect representations and subsequent misunderstandings. The newly discovered silk manuscripts also show a different structure of the text and another succession of chapters, a fact that ultimately leads to giving the work a different title: Te Tao, or—in keeping with its status as "Classic Book"—Te Tao Ching.

Literature

Aside from the **Bible** and the **Bhagavadgita**, the Tao-te Ching is the most-translated work ever, and more translations are published regularly. The following is a small selection of texts only.

Tao-te Ching. A portrait, albeit fictional, of the great Chinese sage Lao-tzu (c. 580–500 B.C.E.), generally believed to be the author of the Tao-te Ching.

Chang, Chung-Yuan, trans. *Tao: A New Way of Thinking. A Translation of the Tao Te Ching.* New York: Harper & Row, 1975.

Feng, Gia-fu, and Jane English, trans. *Tao Te Ching.* New York: Knopf, 1972.

Lau, D. C., trans. *Lao Tzu: Tao Te Ching.* London: Viking, 1963.

Legge, James, trans. *The Sacred Books of China: The Texts of Taoism.* 2 vols. New York: Dover Publications, 1962.

Mair, Victor H., trans. *Tao Te Ching: The Classic Book of Integrity and the Way. A New Translation Based on the Recently Discovered Mawang-tui Manuscripts.* New York: Bantam Books, 1990.

Waley, Arthur, trans. *Lao-Tzu: The Way and Its Power. A Study of the Tao Te Ching and Its Place in Chinese Thought.* London: Allen & Unwin, 1934. Reprint 1977.

Mahavamsa

◆

Written in *Pali, this Great Chronicle is basically a historical record of the development of Buddhism in Sri Lanka (Ceylon), covering the period beginning with the historical Buddha, the sixth and fifth century B.C.E., until about the fourth century C.E.

This poetic history was first put into writing by the monk Mahanama in the sixth century, but his Mahavamsa of three thousand verses was only a beginning; Mahanama has had many successors. A unique feature of this epic is the fact that it was continued by generations of monks up until the year 1956. Since 1977, a group of historians and Pali scholars has once more been occupied with putting the modern and contemporary history of Sri Lanka into poetic verse, thus keeping the Mahavamsa alive for what is now more than twenty-five hundred years.

Another, similar, chronicle in Pali is the Dipavamsa.

Literature
Geiger, Wilhem, and H. M. Bode. *The Dipavamsa and Mahavamsa.* Colombo, Sri Lanka: Cottle, 1908.

Second Shelf
500 B.C.E.–500 C.E.

Mahabharata
Orphic Hymns
Confucian Canon
Tripitaka (or Tipitaka)
Brahmajala Sutra
Dhammapada
Angas
Avadhutagita
Lieh-tzu
Chuang-tzu
Bhagavadgita
Hymns to Isis
Chinese Classics
Nei P'ing
Ashtavakra Samhita
Apocrypha and Pseudepigraphia of the Old Testament
Dead Sea Scrolls
Ramayana
Prajnaparamita Sutra
Diamond Sutra
Heart Sutra
Kojiki
Nihon Shoki (or Nihongi)
Corpus Hermeticum

---◆---

Avadanas
New Testament
Nag Hammadi Scriptures
Apocryphic Gospels of the New Testament
Amitayurdhyana Sutra
Mishnah
Lotus Sutra
Buddha Charita
Pistis Sophia
Sepher ha Razim
Shata Shastra
Huang-t'ing Ching
Tao-tsang
Pop Wuj
Bible
Talmud
Guhyasamaja Tantra
Mahayana-samparigraha
Avatamsaka Sutra
Denkart
Puranas
Midrash
Abhidharmakosha
Devi Mahatmya

Mahabharata. A scene from the Mahabharata showing the heavenly deities as spectators to the great battle. The central figures are Arjuna and Krishna in their chariot.

Mahabharata

♦

The "Great Story of the Bharatas" is a collection of texts compiled in the period from about 540 B.C.E. to the third century C.E., and it is essentially concerned with recounting the legends of the Bharatas (Skt., "raiders" or "plunderers"), an Aryan tribal group, and their descendants. Like the Ramayana, the Mahabharata should be regarded as being mainly a literary work, but the different texts contain much information on religious and spiritual matters, especially in the form of legends centering on yogis and divine teachers. Most of the available manuscripts of this work do contain the Bhagavadgita, as the sixth book, and even recount parts of the later Ramayana.

The work, or rather the compilation of various texts and traditions into a whole, is often attributed to a sage named Vyasa. Vyasa, a legendary—and perhaps entirely fictional—author, has also been credited with writing most of India's sacred literature, including the Vedas and the eighteen Puranas.

The Mahabharata commands such respect and authority that it has sometimes been called the "fifth Veda."

Literature

Buck, Wilhelm, trans. *The Mahabharata*. Berkeley, Calif.: University of California Press, 1973.

Dutt, Romesh Chunder. *The Ramayana, and the Mahabharata: Condensed into English Verse*. New York: E.P. Dutton, 1910. Reprint 1969.

Orphic Hymns

♦

The name Orphic Hymns has been given to a collection of eighty-seven hymns that probably originated in Pergamum, Greece. Authorship of the texts is unknown and dating has proved difficult, but they seem to have been composed around the second and/or first century B.C.E., although they include concepts and elements that are much older. The hymns, highly syncretic in nature, address well-known Greek gods and goddesses such as Dionysus and Demeter, Semele and Adonis. Presumably the hymns were chanted during the *Orphic Mysteries, the initiation ceremonies of a syncretic religion sometimes called Orphism.

Literature
Athanassakis, Apostolos N., trans. *The Orphic Hymns: Text, Translation, and Notes*. Missoula, Mont.: Scholars, 1977.

Confucian Canon

♦

This collection of nine distinctive texts was put into its present form under the guidance of Chu Hsi (1130–1200 C.E.) in the late twelfth century. The canon officially consists of China's so-called Five Classics (Chin., Wu Ching), often falsely attributed to K'ung-tzu, or Confucius (551–479 B.C.E.), and the so-called Four Books (Chin., Ssu Shu), posthumous recordings of the master's sayings and expositions of his ideas by others.

For a discussion of the first five works see **Chinese Classics**. Of the four other books that truly belong to the Confucian Canon, only the Lun Yü (Analects) can be regarded as a reliable source for the actual words of K'ung-tzu. The remaining works originate with other authors who expounded the Confucian teachings. This does not lessen their importance, but these authors did make their own contributions, and probably introduced changes, to the original material as taught by the great Chinese thinker.

Lun Yü (Chin., "selected sayings"), also known as the Analects, represents the teachings and sayings of the scholar, philosopher, and politician K'ung-tzu, or Confucius. Following the master's death in 479 B.C.E., these selected sayings were recorded and compiled by a number of his pupils, an undertaking that took about seventy years. Of all the works attributed to K'ung-tzu, the Lun Yü is probably the one that is most truly his, although we must—as is so often the case with works of such early times—take his students' words for it.

The second book in the Confucian Canon, Meng-tzu, is named after its author, the Confucian philosopher Meng-tzu, also known as Meng K'o or Mencius (371–289 B.C.E.). His writings depart from the idealistic point of view, held by other Confucian thinkers, that humans are intrisically good and have a natural sense of what is right and wrong, which is the major quality that distinguishes them from the other animals. Meng-tzu, who could be described as an early social psychologist, also recognized that education and environment are important factors in each person's individual development.

Ta Hsüeh (Chin., "education for adults") is best known in the West under its title The Great Learning. The basis of this work is one specific chapter of the Li Ching, or Book of Rites (see **Chinese Classics**). The text underwent several editions, rearrangements, and additions at the hand of several authors until it achieved its present form in an edition made by Chu Hsi. Since then the work has for centuries been required reading for all so-called educated men and all civil servants in China. The text has been variously dated from 500 to 200 B.C.E., and the discussion is not yet closed.

The Chung Yung (Chin., "doctrine of the mean"), as with the Ta Hsüeh, is a Confucian elaboration of a single chapter in the Li Ching; similar too was the work's standing in pre-Communist China. However, where the Ta Hsüeh is rational and oriented toward politics and social customs, the Chung Yung is concerned with psychology, religion, and mysticism. There is no generally accepted dating and its present form, again, dates back to Chu Hsi.

Literature

Chai, Ch'u, and Winberg Chai, trans. *The Sacred Books of Confucius, and Other Confucian Classics.* 6 vols. New Hyde Park, N.Y.: University Books, 1965.

Legge, James, trans. *The Four Books: Confucian Analects, The Great Learning, The Doctrine of the Mean, and The Works of Mencius.* New York: Paragon Book Reprint Corp., 1966.

Waley, Arthur, trans. *The Analects of Confucius.* London: Allen & Unwin, 1938. New York: Random House, 1967.

Tripitaka (or Tipitaka)

♦

The terms Tripitaka (*Sanskrit) and Tipitaka (*Pali) both translate as "The Three Baskets" and refer to the canon of scriptures at the heart of all Buddhist schools, but especially that of Theravada (*Hinayana) Buddhism. Only a version written in Pali, the so-called Pali Canon, has been entirely preserved, but a large portion of the texts are also available in a Sanskrit version, and a lesser number are available in Chinese. This essential Buddhist canon is subdivided into three distinct parts, or "baskets": 1) Sutra Pitaka (Pali, Sutta Pitaka); 2) Vinaya Pitka; and 3) Abhidharma.

The Sutra Pitka, or Basket of Writings, describes the last forty years of the life and teachings of Siddhartha Gautama Shakyamuni Buddha and contains the recorded discourses of the master. The Hinayana/Pali edition knows five different sections, each designated as *nikaya* ("assemblage, collection"), whereas the Sanskrit and Chinese *Mahayana editions know only the first four of these, each of which is called an **Agama.**

1. Dirghagama (Skt.), or Digha-nikaya (Pali): the "long collection" of thirty (Mahayana) or thirty-four (Hinayana) *sutras,* twenty-seven of which are common to both schools. The various *sutras* deal with non-Buddhist beliefs and teachings of the time, as well as with the last weeks of the historical Buddha's life and the merits of monastic life. This collection also includes the **Brahmajala Sutra.**

2. Madhyamagama (Skt.), or Majjhima-nikaya (Pali): the "medium collection," also known as the "middle-length sayings," texts mainly concerned with Buddhist metaphysics.

3. Samyuktagama (Skt.), or Samyutta-nikaya (Pali): the "miscellaneous collection" dealing with a variety of topics. It is especially interesting for its teachings concerning meditation.

4. Ekottaragama/Ekottarikagama (Skt., "numerical collection") or Anguttara-nikaya (Pali, "graduated collection").

5. Khuddaka-nikaya (Pali, "short collection"): fifteen short texts, among which we also find the **Dhammapada.**

The Vinaya Pitaka, the Basket of Discipline, contains detailed rules and regulations for the communal life of monks and nuns (with many more rules for nuns than for monks) and guidelines for suitable punishment in cases of murder, rape, theft, slander, lying, and so forth. The texts also regulate food and dress throughout the seasons, as well as times and types of ceremonies. Different schools have slightly different texts of the Vinaya Pitaka. A Chinese translation was made as early as 105 C.E.

The Abhidharma (Pali, Abhidhamma), or Basket of Special Teachings, is a compilation of the earliest texts of Buddhist philosophy and psychology—that is, on training the mind. The Abhidharma texts mainly describe and analyze the spiritual/psychological phenomena contained in the Buddha's teachings, focusing especially on the concepts of self and ego and on how the self is intertwined with reality.

Although these teachings form the actual basis for both the southern Hinayana and northern Mahayana schools, considerable differences exist between the Pali (Theravada, Hinayana) and the Sanskrit (Mahayana-oriented) translations and interpretations of the Abhidarma's seven books:

Pali	Sanskrit
Dhammasangani	Sangitiparyaya
Vibhanga	Dharmaskandha
Kathavatthu	Prajnaptishastra
Puggalapannati	Vijnanakaya
Dhatukatha	Dhatukaya
Yamaka	Prakarana
Patthana	Jnanaprasthana

See also **Abhidhammattha-sangaha** and **Abhidharmakosha**. Sometimes the name Tripitaka is also used for the Chinese collection of scriptures known in Chinese as **San-tsang**.

Literature
Horner, I. B., trans. *The Collection of the Middle Length Sayings (Majjhima-Nikaya)*. 3 vols. London: Pali Text Society, 1954–1959.

Rhys-Davids, Caroline, trans. *Abhidamma Pitaka: A Buddhist Manual of Psychological Ethics*. London: Pali Text Society, 1974.

Rhys-Davids, T. W., and Caroline Rhys-Davids, trans. *Dialogues of the Buddha*. 3 vols. London and Boston: Shambhala, 1977.

Brahmajala Sutra

♦

This text forms an important part of the Dirghagama, the "long collection" of the **Tripitaka**. Although of Indian origin and first written in *Pali, where its title is Brahmajala Sutta, the *sutra* has grown to be of major significance to the development of monastic *Buddhism in China and Japan. The Japanese name for this text is Bommo Sutra.

The *Mahayana version of this Sutra of the Net of Brahman, extant in Chinese, contains the most important rules obligatory for a follower of that branch of Buddhism. The ten major and forty-eight minor injunctions listed in this text constitute the so-called *bodhisattva vow a monk or nun takes after his or her ordination.

For literature, see Tripitaka.

Dhammapada

♦

Officially, the Dhammapada—a collection of teachings written in *Pali— was recognized by the Council of Ashoka (240 B.C.E.) as the sayings of the historical Buddha, and it is part of the Sutra Pitaka (see **Tripitaka**). Like many other such texts, however, this collection of 426 verses in 26 chapters must be recognized as merely representing a particular version of the Buddha's teachings as they were written down a few generations after his death—after about two hundred and fifty years of oral transmission. The work, much valued in the countries adhering to *Theravada Buddhism, encourages its readers to work on achieving salvation and liberation by

Dhammapada. *A traditional statue of the Buddha. The gesture made with his hands indicates that he is preaching. Sarnath, India, fifth century.*

their own efforts rather than by relying on any external teacher, authority, or savior.

Literature

Dhammapada: Translation of Dharma Verses. Translation into English from the Tibetan by the Dharma Publishing Staff. Berkeley, Calif.: Dharma Publishing, 1985.

Easwaran, Eknath, trans. *The Dhammapada*. London: Arkana, 1986.

Müller, Max, trans. *The Dhammapada*. Oxford: Clarendon Press, 1881. Reprint. Delhi: Motilal Banarsidass, 1965.

Angas

♦

These are the sacred writings of the *Jaina religion that record the teachings of the Indian ascetic Vardhamana (540–468 B.C.E.), better known as Mahavira (Skt., "great hero") and regarded as the latest of a series of saints and seers. The Angas (Skt., "limb, part") were written in *Prakrit and did not achieve their final form until the fifth century. The texts deal especially with the concept of karma and with the strict Jainist ethical code requiring absolute noninjury of any living beings: this includes strict vegetarianism and an avoidance of killing even the most annoying insects or the worms one may accidentally tread upon.

Literature

Jacobi, Hermann, trans. *Jaina Sutras*. 2 vols. Sacred Books of the East series, Max Müller, ed., vols. 22, 45. Oxford: Clarendon Press, 1884–1895. Reprint. Delhi: Motilal Banarsidass, 1968.

Avadhutagita

♦

This "song of an illumined one" is a short work by Mahatma Dattatreya (fourth century B.C.E.), about whom little else is known. It extols the way of life of the spiritual adept who has cast off all worldly concerns (Skt., *avadhuta*), who disregards all social conventions, and who lives toward self-realization only.

The text is neither well known nor considered very important, yet its author has succeeded in summarizing the major thoughts and the spirit of the Upanishads and of *Advaita Vedanta, which makes the work interesting to the advanced student of Vedic *Hinduism.

Lieh-tzu

♦

This is one of the major Taoist classics, named after its author Lieh-tzu (c. 350 B.C.E.). Apart from its typically Chinese Taoist concern with immortality, the work speaks mainly of the essential unity of all things and of the futility of human efforts. According to Lieh-tzu, human beings should surrender themselves to the universal flow and relax in accordance to the principles of nature, of Heaven and Earth. The text draws on ancient myth, folktales, and other texts known at the time. The work contains references to the I Ching, the Tao-te Ching, and books belonging to the Confucian Canon.

The author's name and the work's title are sometimes transliterated as Lie-zi or Liä Dsi.

Literature
Giles, Lionel, trans. *Taoist Teachings from the Book of Lieh Tzu*. London: J. Murray, 1912.

Chuang-tzu

♦

One of the major books of *Taoism, the work has become known by the name of its author and inspirer (Chuang-tzu, c. 369–286 B.C.E.) rather than by its Chinese name, Nan-hua chen-ching, or the Divine Classic of Nan-hua.

Although the Inner Chapters were written in about 340 B.C.E., the book itself was not canonized until a thousand years later, in the year 742 C.E. The text consists of thirty-three chapters, of which only the first seven, the Inner Chapters, were actually written by Chuang-tzu. The remaining fifteen "outer" and eleven "mixed" books are the works of his students.

The work stresses the importance of spiritual discipline and a life in accordance with nature. Chuang-tzu disregards the formal conventions represented by K'ung-tzu's philosophy (see **Confucian Canon**) and instead advocates an advanced form of meditation, in which the practitioner meditates on the formless *Tao.

Literature

Feng, Gia-fu, and Jane English, trans. *Chuang Tzu: Inner Chapters*. New York: Vintage, 1974.

Legge, James, trans. *The Sacred Books of China: The Texts of Taoism*. 2 vols. New York: Dover Publications, 1962.

Watson, Burton, trans. *Chuang Tzu: Basic Writings*. New York: Columbia University Press, 1964.

———. *Chuang Tzu: The Complete Works*. New York: Columbia University Press, 1968.

Bhagavadgita

♦

This well-known and popular Song of the Exalted One, or Song of the Lord, in fact merely constitutes the sixth book of the **Mahabharata,** yet it has become the most widely read and famous of all Hindu/Yogic scriptures. The *gita* (Skt., "song") seems to have been composed during the fourth or third century B.C.E., although both earlier and later dates are sometimes given.

Set against the background of a battle between kinsmen, the text is mainly a dialogue between the god Krishna and his student and warrior Arjuna, with extensive discussions of such classic virtues as selflessness, duty, devotion, true knowledge, and meditation. Arjuna is taught "to do what he has to do," but simultaneously to remain unattached and unsoiled by renouncing the consequences of his actions. A universally valid pearl of wisdom from the Bhagavadgita is the statement: "Man is made by his belief. As he believes, so he is."

Although the text is read and venerated by most schools of *Hinduism, it bears clear marks of having originated with the adherents of the *pancaratra* tradition (see *Shaiva). Its tone, however, is rather eclectic, and the authors have apparently tried to integrate several different philosophies and beliefs prevalent at the time of its composition.

Literature

There are many translations of the Bhagavadgita, and more are published regularly. The following is only a small selection of texts.

Radhakrishnan, Sarvepalli. *The Bhagavadgita.* London: Routledge & Kegan Paul, 1948. Reprint 1960.

Zachner, R. C. *The Bhagavadgita.* Oxford: Clarendon Press, 1969. New York: Oxford University Press, 1973.

Hymns to Isis

♦

The Hymns to Isis in her temple on the island of Philae constitute an interesting "document" in terms of understanding and appreciating the exalted position of this Egyptian goddess even in the times of Ptolemaic Egypt. The eight hieroglyphic hymns were engraved into the walls of her sanctuary sometime during the years 284 to 246 B.C.E. and were probably recited in daily prayers, during certain religious festivals, or both. Naturally, they represent texts that evolved earlier in time, and parts of the same hymns have been found elsewhere in Egyptian temples. In these texts, Isis is venerated under many names and with many epithets, often combining attributes of various female deities within herself.

This comprehensive Isis, modeled on other and earlier Egyptian and Near Eastern deities such as Hathor, Astarte, and Ishtar, is credited here

Hymns to Isis. *The entire northern wall of room X in the Temple of Isis at Philae is covered with hieroglyphs and images of the goddess.*

and elsewhere with being mother of the universe and creatrix of all gods and of humanity, with smiting evil and ending the practice of cannibalism, with having great magical powers, and with the co-invention of hieroglyphic and demotic writing (with the Greek Hermes), to name but a few of her powers and accomplishments.

The whole Temple of Isis at Philae, probably the largest and heaviest sacred scripture there is, was dismantled after having been submerged in water and was completely rebuilt (1975–1977) on the island of Algilkia.

Literature
Zabkar, Louis V. *Hymns to Isis at Philae.* Hanover, N.H.: University Press of New England, 1988.

Chinese Classics
♦

A major problem concerning these five, and previously six, classical books lies in the fact that the old Chinese manuscripts had been suppressed, and many actually burned in 213 B.C.E., under the emperor Ch'in Shih Huang Ti. Subsequently, a controversy arose between those who rewrote the Chinese Classics in the then-reformed Chinese script and those who used old editions that had purportedly survived the burning. This is mainly of concern to the historian, however, and does not change the essential teachings and wisdom contained in the texts, although alterations have almost certainly been introduced. Consequently, most of the works we now know must be dated, in their written form, to the second and first centuries B.C.E.

The almost legendary classical books of China are often and "officially" regarded as part of the **Confucian Canon**, where they are known as Wu Ching and are sometimes even directly attributed to K'ung-tzu (551–479 B.C.E.). Nonetheless, most of the material in these books dates from pre-Confucian times, and it has been established that K'ung-tzu did not write a single word contained therein. We can therefore better refer to these works simply as Chinese Classics.

1. Shu Ching (Classic of History): The language of this work clearly dates its appearance in written form to not earlier than the Han dynasty (23–220 C.E.), but the documents and speeches contained in the text are attributed to early Chinese rulers. The history speaks of early, almost legendary emperors such as Yao (third millennium B.C.E.) and covers the development of Chinese culture up to about 1000 B.C.E.

2. Shih Ching (Classic of Odes): A verse anthology of three hundred poems and songs that have been dated roughly to the period 1000–500 B.C.E. The collection contains many ritual hymns and folksongs, but also political poems and love songs. In the West, the work is often referred to as the Book of Poetry.

3. I Ching (Classic of Changes): This ancient text, one of the oldest known scriptures, was extended in the second and first centuries B.C.E. with the so-called wings, Confucian commentaries and appendices. See the entry I Ching.

4. Ch'un Ch'iu (Spring and Autumn Annals): A historical record of the state of Lu, thus dating from 722–481 B.C.E., sometimes wrongly attributed to K'ung-tzu as an author or editor rather than, perhaps, as a contributor.

5. Li Ching (Classic of Rites): This work contains the three books Chou Li (Rites of the Chou dynasty), I Li (Ceremonies and Rites), and Li Chi (Record of Rites). The work represents a compilation of texts written down in about 200 B.C.E.; the contents, however, cover Chinese religious practices from the eighth to fifth centuries B.C.E. Two chapters of this work form the basis for two books that belong to the so-called Confucian Canon.

6. Yüeh Ching (Classic of Music): A previously existing sixth classic, referred to in other texts, that is probably lost forever.

Literature

Karlgren, Bernhard. *The Book of Odes*. London: Routledge & Kegan Paul, 1950.

Legge, James. *The Chinese Classics*. Vol. 3: *The Shoo Ching*. Vol. 4: *The*

She Ching. London: Trübner, 1861–1872. Reprint. New York: Krishna, 1935.

———. *The Sacred Books of China: The Texts of Confucianism.* Sacred Books of the East series, Max Müller, ed., vols. 27, 28. Oxford: Clarendon Press, 1879. Reprint. Delhi: Motilal Banarsidass, 1966.

Steele, J. *I Li; or, The Book of Etiquette and Ceremonial.* London: Probsthain, 1917.

Walters, Derek, trans. *The T'ai Hsüan Ching: The Hidden Classic. A Lost Companion of the I Ching.* Wellingborough, England: Thorsons, 1983.

Nei P'ing

♦

This extraordinary text was written by the Chinese scholar and initiate Ko Hung (284–364 C.E.), the first author of the so-called religious branch of *Taoism to break with the taboo against writing down the oral traditions. The Nei P'ing is thus a text rich with comments and discussions of Taoist "secret," alchemical, magical, and psychophysical "recipes," and it represents a selection of Taoist beliefs and practices of the time and earlier. Considering that the so-called religious/magical tradition (Chin., *Tao-chiao*) blossomed in the second century B.C.E., beginning in 220, the Nei P'ing probably contains much from that time.

The work itself, written in 320, still shows these Taoists' general contempt for the written word and especially for the so-called **Chinese Classics**, which are called "straw dogs" and "effigies of the past" (Ware, 1981, p. 328). The work also includes, however, a very interesting and lengthy "Taoist library" —more than one hundred works on silken scrolls that Ko Hung had collected during his studies. On those texts, his teacher once commented: "A large number of volumes of the various Taoist writings are bound to contain something valuable, but . . . don't waste your time and overwork your mind by learning all of them completely" (Ware, 1981, p. 312).

See also the quote (Ware, 1981, p. 328) at the beginning of this book.

Literature

Ware, James R. *Alchemy, Medicine, and Religion in the China of A.D. 320: The Nei P'ien of Ko Hung.* Cambridge, Mass.: MIT Press, 1966. New York: Dover Publications, 1981.

Ashtavakra Samhita

♦

Also known as Ashtavakragita, this is one of the earliest works belonging to the literature of the **Samhitas.** Considered to be a standard work of *Advaita Vedanta, the short text explores and describes the various perceptions and concepts of *Vedanta. The text is attributed to Ashtavakra (second century B.C.E.), the crippled sage who, despite his physical handicap, was also the principal teacher of Patanjali (see **Yoga Sutra**).

Apocrypha and Pseudepigraphia of the Old Testament

♦

These represent a number of books that were declared "uninspired" and were excluded from the Hebrew Bible (see **Old Testament**) as well as from most Christian versions of the **Bible.**

The apocryphal books (apocrypha means "hidden things") pertaining to the Old Testament consist of sixteen books written in Greek during the last two centuries B.C.E. They provide us with information on the cultural environment during the period shortly before the coming of Christianity. Most of these were originally included in the Greek Septuagint but not in the Hebrew Bible. After the canonization of these texts by the Catholic church in 1546, they were printed in the King James Version of the Bible, between the Old and New Testaments; this is why the texts are also referred to as intertestamental literature. The scriptures in question were excluded from that Book of Books once again after 1629; they were never accepted by the Protestant churches.

The Old Testamentarian Apocrypha consist of such works as Books 3 and 4 of Ezra, the Book of Baruch, and the Book of Judith, to name but a few.

Most of the pseudepigraphic works are of a later date, texts often ascribed to ancient figures such as Enoch/Henoch (third millennium B.C.E.), Moses (c. 1000 B.C.E.), and other early patriarchs of Israel. The discovery of the so-called **Dead Sea Scrolls** of Qumran have updated our knowledge of the intertestamental literature, and it now seems that most of the pseudepigraphia, in the words of one of their discoverers, are "closely connected with, if not emanating from" the Essene sect at Qumran (Allegro, 1982, p. 128). Whether or not the books represent oral traditions that go back to the ancient sages, or whether they are simply and falsely ascribed to them, remains to be studied by scholars, archaeologists, and historians. Among the pseudepigraphic writings are such texts as the Testaments of, respectively, Abraham, Adam, and Job; the Ladder of Jacob; and also the Apocalypses of Adam, Abraham, Baruch, and Ezra. A text known as Sibylline Oracles is connected to the **Sibylline Books.**

Literature

Charles, R. H., ed. *The Apocrypha and Pseudepigraphia of the Old Testament in English.* 2 vols. London: Oxford University Press, 1913. Reprint 1968.

Harris, J. R., and A. A. Mingana, eds. *The Odes and Psalms of Solomon.* 2 vols. Manchester, England: Manchester University Press, 1916–1920.

Metzger, Bruce M., ed. *The Oxford Annotated Apocrypha.* New York: Oxford, 1965.

Russell, D. S. *The Old Testament Pseudepigraphia: Patriarchs and Prophets in Early Judaism.* London: SCM Press, 1987.

Dead Sea Scrolls

♦

Since their discovery (1947–1956), the scrolls found at Qumran have become truly famous. They date from the period 150 B.C.E. to 68 C.E., the year the scrolls were hidden just before the local Essene community—sometimes called "a breakaway Jewish sect"—was destroyed. These dates, at first considered to be tentative and controversial, were confirmed in Jerusalem in 1990 by carbon-14 dating.

Apart from texts that also form part of the Biblical Old Testament, the scrolls contain hymns, philosophical treatises, and a manual concerning life and discipline in the Essene community. An especially controversial thesis based on this find is that both John the Baptist and Jesus (c. 7 B.C.E.–c. 33 C.E.) may have been members of the Essenes.

The texts, once they have been published in their entirety, could enlarge

Dead Sea Scrolls.
A sample of the so-called
Dead Sea Scolls found
at Qumran between 1947
and 1956.

our understanding of the cultural and religious climate before and during the early development of Christianity, and especially add to our knowledge of the writings usually known as intertestamental literature (see **Apocrypha and Pseudepigraphia of the Old Testament**). Even now, however, more than forty years after their discovery, the texts have not yet been fully translated and have become generally accessible only in 1991. In *The Dead Sea Scrolls Deception,* authors Michael Baigent and Richard Leigh reported that the select group working on that task, all members of the Roman

Catholic Ecole Biblique, had always denied independent researchers any access whatsoever to the scrolls.

Literature
Allegro, John M. *The Dead Sea Scrolls: A Reappraisal.* 2nd ed. Harmondsworth, England: Penguin, 1964. Reprint 1982.
Vermes, G., ed. and trans. *The Dead Sea Scrolls in English.* Harmondsworth, England: Penguin, 1962. New York: Heritage, 1967.

Ramayana
♦

Along with the **Mahabharata,** the Ramayana (Skt., "life of Rama") is one of the two major national epics of Indian literature. The Indian version, attributed to the poet and sage Valmiki, was compiled at some time during the first century B.C.E., although its preliterate roots go back six or seven centuries earlier. A much later, Javanese version (from 1094 C.E., in Java, Indonesia) also exists, a version attributed to Yogisvara (eleventh century C.E.).

The work, consisting of seven chapters and more than twenty thousand stanzas, has several dimensions. It is not only an Indian story of a tragic love—between Rama and Sita—but is also an epic dealing with the asceticism so typical for India. As a whole, the Ramayana is an interesting repository of folklore, moral values, and folk wisdom. Even today, most of India's rural and often illiterate population knows the Ramayana; learned mainly through recitations and public readings, the work nevertheless remains a primary source for religious and moral concepts.

Literature
Buck, Wilhelm. *Ramayana: King Rama's Way.* Berkeley, Calif.: University of California Press, 1976.
Dutt, Romesh Chunder. *The Ramayana, and the Mahabharata: Condensed into English Verse.* New York: Dutton, 1910. Reprint 1969.

Prajnaparamita Sutra

◆

The Prajnaparamita Sutra is an important collection of forty *sutras,* the name of which can be translated as Supreme Essence or Great Transcendental Wisdom. The *sutra* was composed around the beginning of the common era and was translated into Chinese as early as the year 179. It is regarded as one of the *Vaipulya *sutras* of *Mahayana.

The individual *sutras* vary in length from short texts of a mere three hundred verses to huge works of one hundred thousand verses. Probably the oldest part of the collection is the Ashtasahasrika, a composition of eight thousand verses that recall discussions between the Buddha and his students and disciples.

The collection as a whole has had a great impact on the development of Buddhist and other Eastern (religious) schools of thought, and some of its individual texts have achieved great importance and fame by themselves. Among these, probably the best-known individual *sutras,* at least in the West, are the **Diamond Sutra** and the **Heart Sutra.** The Prajnaparamita is also part of the Chinese **San-tsang** collection of Buddhist texts.

Literature

Conze, Edward, trans. *The Perfection of Wisdom in Eight Thousand Lines.* Berkeley, Calif.: Four Seasons/Grey, 1973.

———. *The Short Prajanaparamita Texts.* London: Luzac, 1973.

Lancaster, Lewis R., ed. *Prajnaparamita and Related Systems: Studies in Honor of Edward Conze.* Berkeley, Calif.: University of California Press, 1977.

Diamond Sutra

◆

The Diamond Cutter of Supreme Wisdom, part of the **Prajnaparamita Sutra,** this text has become especially influential among the *Mahayana

Diamond Sutra. A page from the world's first printed book (China, 868 C.E.), a Chinese translation of the Diamond Sutra.

schools of Tibet, China, and Japan. The philosophical and psychological work is famous for its diamondlike sharpness, which, in the *sutra*'s words, "cuts away all unnecessary conceptualizations" about the nature of reality, exposing all phenomenal appearances as projections of the mind only. The Diamond Sutra was the first book ever to be printed, a celebrated event that occurred in China, in the year 868. The text ends by saying that it leads the serious student "to the other shore of enlightenment."

The *Sanskrit title of this text is Vajrachchedika-prajnaparamita Sutra; it is known in Japan as Kongo-kyo.

Literature

Conze, Edward, trans. *Buddhist Wisdom Books, Containing the Diamond Sutra and the Heart Sutra.* London: Allen & Unwin, 1958. Reprint 1970.

Price, A.F., trans. and Mou-lam Wong. *The Diamond Sutra and the Sutra of Hui Neng.* Boston: Shambhala, 1969. Reprint 1985.

Heart Sutra

◆

This shortest *sutra* of the **Prajnaparamita Sutra** is held in high regard in China and Japan, especially among *Zen practitioners who see it as the "heart" of the Prajnaparamita and as one of the most important Buddhist texts. It contains the quintessential and often-quoted statement that "form is no other than emptiness; emptiness is no other than form." The *sutra's* complete *Sanskrit title is Mahapraj- naparamita-hridaya Sutra; it is known in Japan as Hannya Shingyo, short for Maka Hannyaharamita Shingyo.

Literature

Chang, Garma C. C., trans. *The Buddhist Teaching of Totality: The Philosophy of Hwa Yen Buddhism*. University Park, Pa., and London: Pennsylvania State University Press, 1971.

Conze, Edward, trans. *Buddhist Wisdom Books, Containing the Diamond Sutra and the Heart Sutra*. London: Allen & Unwin, 1958. Reprint 1970.

Thomas, E. J., trans. *The Perfection of Wisdom: A Selection of Mahayana Scriptures*. London: Murray, 1952. Reprint. Westport, Conn.: Greenwood Press, 1979.

Kojiki

◆

This is the oldest work in the Japanese language, the title of which translates as Records of Ancient Matters. The text was presented to the Japanese Imperial Court in 712 and must have been written mainly during the seventh and the early eighth centuries, although undoubtedly it contains teachings and imagery that are much older. Together with the **Nihon Shoki,** the Kojiki forms the scriptural basis of non-Buddhist, Japanese belief and is probably the most important document of *Shinto religion and mythology.

The cosmological speculations of the Kojiki are heavily dependent on Chinese concepts, but the text also sets forth such specifically Japanese myths as the creation of the world and of Japan by the deities Izanagi and

Izanami along with the stories concerning the sun goddess Amaterasu; her aggressive, rapist brother Susano-o; and the wild, spontaneous goddess Ama-no-Uzume. Apart from such myth and legends, the text provides insight into the customs, ceremonies, and observances of early Japan.

Considering that an organized Shinto religion is generally ascribed to the first century, the traditions of the Kojiki and the Nihon Shoki are at least as old as that.

Literature
Chamberlain, B. H., trans. *Kojiki; or, Records of Ancient Matters*. Tokyo: Transactions of the Asiatic Society of Japan, vol. 10, supplement, 1882.

Nihon Shoki (or Nihongi)
♦

These Chronicles of Japan, like the Kojiki, contain many of Japan's most ancient myths and legends, which often deal with the transference of power from the divine to the human realm, especially to the Imperial Court. Together with the Kojiki, the Nihon Shoki, written in 720, forms the basis of original and contemporary *Shinto beliefs, and its teachings have also been used to feed Japanese nationalism, for example, before and during World War II.

Considering that an organized Shinto religion is generally ascribed to the first century, the Nihon Shoki's traditions are at least as old as that.

Literature
Aston, W. G. *Nihongi: Chronicles of Japan from the Earliest Times to* A.D. *697*. London: Allen & Unwin, 1956.

Corpus Hermeticum
♦

This is the title for a collection of seventeen chapters, or tractates, of hermetic writings originating in Alexandria during the first two or three

Corpus Hermeticum. This section of pavement in the Siena Cathedral (fifteenth century) shows that the teachings of Thrice Great Hermes were known to the master Masons and were greatly appreciated. This essentially "pagan" tradition thus found its way into Christian places of worship and sometimes into the minds of enlightened Christian thinkers.

centuries of the common era. Most famous among them is the first chapter, the so-called Divine Pymander, or Poimandres ("shepherd of men"), the title of which has sometimes been used as a title for the complete collection.

Traditionally this and other texts of the Corpus are attributed to a legendary and/or divine teacher, Hermes Trismegistus. This "Thrice Great Hermes," or "Thrice Great Thoth," where Hermes (Greek) and Thoth (Egyptian) are the respective names for the same god of writing and wisdom, has sometimes been regarded as a human teacher, although there is no real evidence for this. The different opinions and teachings presented in the text indicate that they probably originate with different authors, some of whom were more or less *Gnostics, with others belonging to one of the various syncretic religious movements of the time; the teachings of these "esoteric brotherhoods" were a mixture of Egyptian, Greek, and Jewish wisdom and mysticism. What the texts have in common is their call for the individual to raise his or her consciousness, promoting a spirituality that values direct, personal experience above belief in any authority.

Some of these texts have also been found among the **Nag Hammadi Scriptures**, the *Coptic translation of which threw new light on the originally Greek texts.

Literature
Scott, Walter, ed. and trans. *Hermetica: The Ancient Greek and Latin Writings Which Contain Religious or Philosophic Teachings Ascribed to Hermes Trismegistus.* 4 vols. Oxford: Clarendon Press, 1924–1936. Reprint. Boston: Shambhala, 1983–1985.

Avadanas
♦

The term *avadana* (Skt., "great deed") indicates a specific type of Buddhist literature from the early centuries C.E. Written during the time that *Hinayana was giving rise to the first *Mahayana schools, the texts in question often contain glorification of the then-new *bodhisattva ideal. Two of the best-known and most popular texts are the Avadanashataka (One Hundred Heroic Deeds) and the Divyavadana (Divine Deeds). The texts mainly contain allegorical legends concerning the great deeds of Buddhist "saints."

New Testament

♦

This is the collective name for the twenty-seven later books of the **Bible**, concerned with the life and teachings of Jesus of Nazareth (c. 7 B.C.E.–33 C.E.). The texts were first written in Greek, including the translations of the probably *Aramaic sayings of Jesus himself. This part of the **Bible**, including the Gospels, the Acts of the Apostles, the Revelation of St. John and several epistles, is the truly Christian part of the Book of Books and is not found in Hebrew/Jewish versions.

In the New Testament we also read about the Christian apostle's crusade against the so-called heathens—about their fight against the old religions, which often worshipped female deities. Paul, for example, as reported in the Acts, tried to end the veneration of the goddess Artemis/Diana. John, on the other hand, wrote these famous words in an attempt to discredit the worshipers of the goddess: "I saw a woman sit upon a scarlet coloured beast, full of names of blasphemy, having seven heads and ten horns. And the woman was arrayed in purple and scarlet colour, and decked with gold and precious stones and pearls, having a golden cup in her hand full of abominations" (Revelation 17: 3–4).

Nag Hammadi Scriptures

♦

Discovered in 1945 at Nag Hammadi, a town along the Nile of Upper Egypt, these documents are fifty-three mostly *Coptic texts written in the fourth century and often translated from earlier Greek originals. The scriptures were found in thirteen leather-bound papyrus codices. These texts have since been fully translated into modern languages, and we can

New Testament. An elaborate title page to the gospel of St. Luke.
From the Lindesfarne gospel book.

therefore study the teachings of various Gnostic schools without having to rely on the word of those who consider those schools to be merely another group of heretics.

The Nag Hammadi texts that have been best known, although these are not necessarily the most important, are the Gospel of Truth, the Gospel According to Thomas, and the Gospel of Philip. A short, second-century Gospel According to Mary (Magdalene) is of special interest in that it establishes the existence of esoteric teachings given by Jesus and the fact that in this case a woman was given the authority to teach. Furthermore, the papyri contain portions of Plato's writings, cosmological speculations, and hermetic and mystic teachings including concepts and techniques concerning ritual and/or spiritual sexuality. The so-called Jung Codex, named after its owner C. G. Jung (1875–1961), is also part of the Nag Hammadi collection.

The Nag Hammadi documents, which are not complete (some seem to have been burned in the oven of a poor and unknowing Egyptian woman), are also known as Chenoboskion manuscripts, so named after a monastery nearby Nag Hammadi.

Literature

Robinson, James M., ed. *The Nag Hammadi Library*. 3rd ed., rev. Leiden and New York: Brill, 1988.

Apocryphic Gospels of the New Testament

♦

As does the Old Testament, the New Testament knows a number of apocrypha. These are gospels (Old English for "good tidings") similar to those of the official canon, but excluded by early Christian censors. Such gospels appeared beginning in about the year 150, and claimed—sometimes perhaps legitimately—to represent the more "esoteric" teachings of Jesus given in private to individual apostles and such personal friends as Mary Magdalene, whom he "loved more than the rest of woman" (Robinson, 1988, p. 525; see Nag Hammadi Scriptures).

Whereas the canon of the New Testament recognizes only four gospels, several more are recognized among the apocryphic texts—for example the Gospel of the Egyptians and that of the Hebrews, as well as a Gospel of Petrus and one of Nicodemus. Many more texts such as these, not all gospels, constitute what are called the New Testamentarian apocrypha, all of which have been translated and are presently available in many languages.

For similar works, see also the **Nag Hammadi Scriptures.**

Literature

Hennecke, Edgar, ed. *New Testament Apocrypha.* 2 vols. Translated from the German by A. J. B. Higgins and others. Philadelphia: Westminster Press, 1963–1965.

James, M. R., ed. and trans. *The Apocryphal New Testament, Being the Apocryphal Gospels, Acts, Epistles, and Apocalypses, with Other Narrative Fragments.* Oxford: Clarendon Press, 1924.

Amitayurdhyana Sutra

◆

The Sutra on the Contemplation of the Buddha of Boundless Life (Amitayus, or Amitabha) is one of the major texts of the Chinese and Japanese Pure Land schools of *Buddhism, in which the observance of moral rules and the recital of Amitabha's name are the major concerns of ritual practice. The work also explains and teaches a number of visualizations that are considered beneficial and necessary in order to attain rebirth in the Pure Land, the realm of the Buddha. Other texts of this school, founded in 402, are the Amitabha Sutra and the Sukhavati-vyuha, the last two available only in Chinese translations of lost Indian works—for example, in the **San-tsang.**

Mishnah

◆

These are the basic texts of Judaic law, compiled and edited by the rabbi Jehuda Ha-Nasi (b. 135) beginning late in the second century. The texts are known to have been drawn from earlier, oral traditions (going back to about 200 B.C.E.). The collection soon became second in authority only to the Hebrew Bible (**Old Testament**). Together with the Gemara (interpretations and commentaries on the Mishnah texts) the work forms the basis for both the Palestinian and Babylonian **Talmud.**

Literature

Danby, Herbert, trans. *The Mishnah*. London: Oxford University Press, 1933. Reprint 1954.

Lotus Sutra

◆

Known in *Sanskrit as Saddharmapundarika Sutra, this "*sutra* of the lotus of the wonderful law" is recognized as an important text, a *Vaipulya *sutra,* by all schools of *Mahayana Buddhism, but it is particularly venerated by the Chinese T'ien-t'ai (Jap., Tendai) and Hua-yin (Jap., Kegon) schools. The *sutra* is known in Chinese as Wu-liang I Ching and in Japanese as Hokke-kyo.

The work is cast in the form of a sermon given by the historical Buddha before an audience consisting of gods, demons, and worldly rulers, and it is said to be the last sermon the teacher gave before reaching enlightenment. It extols the virtue of compassion, the heart of the *bodhisattva ideal, and affirms the possibility for every being to have the potential for Buddhahood.

The Lotus Sutra is the major scripture for Japanese schools such as that founded by Nichiren (1222–1282), and for many of the so-called New Religions that have developed in Japan in the twentieth century.

Literature

The Wonderful Dharma Lotus Flower Sutra. San Francisco, Calif.: Buddhist Text Translation Society, 1974.

Kato, Bunno, with Yoshiro Tamuta and Kojiro Miyasaka, trans. *The Threefold Lotus Sutra*. New York: Weatherhill/Kosei, 1975.

Buddha Charita

◆

The Life of the Buddha is a poetic work by Ashvagosha (c. 200 C.E.), the famous Brahmin who converted to *Buddhism and became an important *Mahayana philosopher.

The twenty-eight songs of this work recount and describe the Buddha's life in heroic and glorifying terms, and the text has been influential in the devotional movement that has, unintentionally, grown up around the figure of Siddharta Gautama, the historical Buddha (563–483 B.C.E.). Only thirteen chapters are extant in its original *Sanskrit version, but the text exists in a Tibetan translation as well.

Pistis Sophia

◆

This, perhaps, is the best-known of Gnostic texts; written in *Coptic, it was discovered in Egypt sometime during the eighteenth century. The text, dated to about the year 250 and first translated into German in 1851, is written as if it represents teachings given directly by Jesus (c. 7 B.C.E.–c. 33 C.E.) after his crucifixion and resurrection.

The Pistis Sophia, which can be translated as "faith wisdom," is a work of the more ascetically oriented school within *Gnosticism. The text associates sexuality with a demon ruler and his cohort and has the alleged Jesus condemn the relevant rituals held by other Gnostics. When the text speaks of the downfall of Sophia ("wisdom" personified as a goddess) from the heavenly spheres and her subsequent exile in the material world, it finds fault, among other things, in Sophia's desire for independence.

Literature
Horner, G. W., ed. *Pistis Sophia*. London: Watkins, 1924.
Mead, George Robert Stow. *Pistis Sophia*. London: Watkins, 1921.

Sepher ha Razim

♦

This Book of Secret Mysteries is a little-known text dating from the third century that contains traditional material on Jewish/Hellenistic magic and incantations, as well as astrological knowledge of the time. The text claims to be of ancient origin and to have been known to Noah and to King Solomon (990–922 B.C.E.). The work most likely was written to preserve knowledge of these ancient arts as such practices became increasing outlawed.

Shata Shastra

♦

This Treatise of the Hundred Songs was important to the development of Buddhism, especially in China. Its author, Aryadeva (third century; also known as Kanadeva), a patriarch in the early lineage of *Ch'an, here refutes the various verbal, philosophical attacks that were made against Buddhism by opposed Chinese schools of thought. The Shata Shastra is a fundamental work in the San-lun school of Chinese *Mahayana.

Huang-t'ing Ching

♦

The title of this third-century Taoist treatise translates as the Classic Treatise of the Yellow Castle; "yellow castle" refers to the human heart.

The Huang-t'ing Ching is designed to be recited, not simply read; the recitation aids in the visualization and invocation of the "body deities" named in the work. The text contains descriptions and instructions concerning *fang-chung shu (sexual techniques), breathing exercises, and other practices aiming at achieving immortality, a pursuit that plays a large role in the inner alchemy of *Taoism.

The text should not be confused with the Huang-ti nei-ching, the Yellow Emperor's famous classical work on Chinese medicine.

Considering the text's early dating, it could have been a medium for the often-discussed Chinese influence on the first Indian *Tantras, texts that appeared three to four hundred years later.

See also **Mahacinacara-sara Tantra.**

Tao-tsang

♦

This is the Chinese term for what is also known as the Taoist Canon, a vast collection of almost fifteen hundred works written during many centuries and originating with a variety of Taoist schools: philosophical and magical, mainstream and heretic. The varied teachings of *Taoism brought together in this collection are difficult to date and do, in fact, belong to various ages. The oldest parts, originally in oral form and in handwritten manuscripts, probably go back to the shamanic tradition of the first and perhaps second millennium B.C.E. As a whole, however, the Taoist Canon probably came into being during the third through fifth centuries C.E., in part as an indigenous Chinese answer to the then-growing influence of *Mahayana Buddhism with its organized body of literature in the form of *sutras* and **Agamas** (see **Tripitaka**).

The first printed edition of the work, produced around 1190, was even larger than described above, but a number of texts were lost when that edition was destroyed in 1281 by order of the Mongol emperor Kublai Khan (1216–1284). The texts that have survived were first reissued in printed form in 1436, during the Ming dynasty (1368–1644). This Tao-tsang comprises 1,464 individual texts in several sections, designated as "caves" (Chin., *tung*). The first section is called the Tung-chen, or "cave of truth"; the second section is Tung-hsuan, or "cave of mystery"; and the third section is Tung-shen, or "cave of spirits." The fourth to sixth sections contain supplements to, respectively, the first to third, while a seventh—called "The Orthodox One" (Chin., *Cheng-i*)—and eighth section containing later, post-Mongol works bring the collection to a close.

The complete work consists of about fifty million Chinese characters in various, sometimes secret "alphabets," and several thousand illustrations and diagrams. The contents range from alchemical writings to text describing the preparation of talismans, from cosmological speculation to medicine, from mythology to ecstatic, visionary, and mystical techniques and insights. At the beginning of the twentieth century only a single edition of the Tao-tsang—kept at a monastery in Peking—was available. In 1926, this edition was photographically reproduced and thus became available for serious studies. The work has as yet not been translated, although this is in progress under the guidance of Kristopher Schipper, an initiated Taoist master and a renowned scholar of Chinese culture, at the École Pratique des Hautes Études (Sciences Religieuses) in Paris. Meanwhile, some information and a great number of images taken from the Tao-tsang—talismanic calligraphy, secret alphabets, and diagrams of the subtle body—can be found, with commentaries, in the literature listed below.

Literature:

Legeza, Laszlo. *Tao Magic: The Secret Language of Diagrams and Calligraphy*. London: Thames & Hudson, 1975. Reprint 1987.

Rawson, Philip, and Laszlo Legeza. *Tao: The Chinese Philosophy of Change*. London: Thames & Hudson, 1973.

Schipper, Kristopher. *Tao: De levende religie van China*. Amsterdam: Meulenhoff, 1988

Pop Wuj

♦

Our knowledge of this book, and most of its translations, is dependent on a version of the text that was recorded between 1554 and 1558 in a Spanish alphabet. Until recently, this sacred Book of Counsel of the Quiche Mayas (Guatemala) was known under the name Popol Vuh. In order to make a new and better translation of this text, which had been distorted by the use of a European alphabet, a new and specifically Quiche-adapted alphabet was invented by Don Adrian Chavez (c. 1900–1987). He added

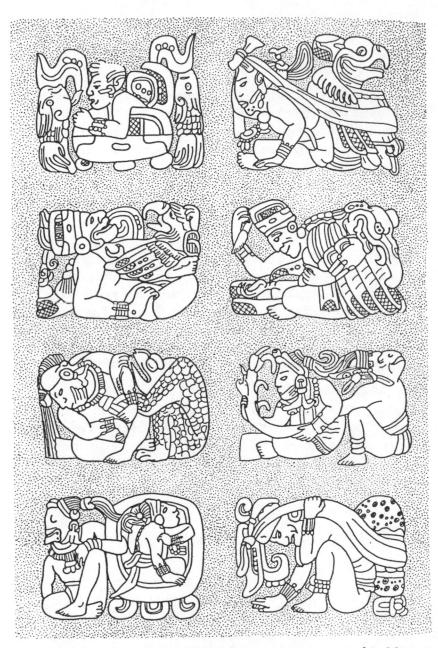

Pop Wuj. *A few samples of the elaborate pictograms used in Mayan writing and counting. The depicted figures represent gods and goddesses from Mayan mythology and religion. Adapted from a stela at Copan.*

seven extra letters to the Roman alphabet in order to create a script that fits Mayan speech, and according to this new alphabet, the text's name is now transliterated as Pop Wuj.

The work was first written down in the pictograms (also called hieroglyphs) typical for Mesoamerica. That version most likely originated during the ninth through the thirteenth centuries and is no longer extant. Its contents, however, carried through time orally, date back at least to the classic period of Mayan civilization (300–900), if not to the Mayas' roots in the Olmec culture.

The work contains the Mayan myths of creation, legends, and spiritual traditions, but it is also a source for exact historical data; for example, it lists the dates of all kings up to the fifteenth century. There are indications that the Pop Wuj, with its beautiful tales of heroes battling the dark forces of the netherworld and its fascinating descriptions of Mayan culture, is only a small part of a larger Mayan epic cycle, of which other parts have been lost and/or destroyed.

See also **Tonalpohualli.**

Literature

Chavez, Don Adrian, trans. *Pop Wuj*. Quetzaltenango, Guatemala, 1980.

Girard, Raphael, trans. *Esotericism of the Popol Vuh*. Pasadena, Calif.: Theosophical University Press, 1979.

Goetz, Delia, and Sylvanus Morley, trans. *Popul Vuh: The Sacred Book of the Ancient Quiche Maya*. Norman, Okla.: University of Oklahoma Press, 1950.

Tedlock, Dennis, trans. *Popol Vuh: The Mayan Book of the Dawn of Life and the Glories of Gods and Kings*. New York: Simon & Schuster, 1986.

Bible

♦

The work known as the Bible actually consists of diverse texts by many authors, written in Hebrew, Greek, and *Aramaic. Some of the texts are almost three thousand years old (**Old Testament**), and they often represent even more ancient oral traditions; they achieved their written form throughout the centuries from about 1000 B.C.E. to approximately 100 C.E. The form in which more than 1.5 billion people today know this so-called Book of Books is based on decisions made during the Council of Nicea (325 C.E.), where the Bible was given its canonical form.

The older and much larger part of the work, the **Old Testament**, offers much source material about the many peoples and religions that once existed in the ancient Near East. It shows the continuous struggle of the then newly developing, monotheistic worship of the god Jahweh, or Jehovah, against the religious beliefs of the peoples of Canaan, Elam, Egypt, and other nations or tribal states. Apart from this Old Testament, written in Hebrew and sometimes called the Hebrew Bible, and the later **New Testament,** written in Greek and recognized by Christians only, some old versions of the Bible also include the **Apocrypha,** texts that later were omitted by most Jewish and Christian schools and sects.

Since the Old Testament had already been translated into Greek (the Septuagint, 285 B.C.E.), a complete Greek Bible circulated throughout the Mediterranean area once the New Testament had been completed in about 100 C.E. Three centuries later, in 404, the Bible also appeared in Latin and as such was called the Vulgate. This led to Latin becoming the liturgical language of the Roman Catholic church for more than fifteen hundred years. The fifteenth and sixteenth centuries brought the first printed Bible, as well as the first translations into the languages of the common people (see The Wheel of Time)—thus undermining the authority of the Catholic church and preparing the way for different interpretations and the foundation of different schools and sects.

There are texts in the Bible that speak to the historian, the anthropologist and psychologist, the political sociologist, and, last but not least, to the faithful of one or another associated system of belief. With its many diverse texts, the Book of Books embraces so much of the human experience that it also has fallen prey to frequent misuse by people from numerous schools and with differing religious and/or political inclinations.

Talmud

♦

This is the major work of postbiblical Jewish literature, codified between the late fourth century (Jerusalem Talmud) and the early sixth century (Babylonian Talmud). It is a written compilation of commentaries on ancient, orally transmitted laws and customs, and it represents a written interpretation of the development of Hebrew thought and tradition.

The Talmud is divided into sections, each concerning different aspects of traditions. Legends, poetry, and anecdotes are found in the Aggada, and legal matters constitute the Halakah. The texts are based on the Mishnah, a second-century work containing the basic laws of Judaism, and the Gemara, third- and fourth-century commentaries on law and social life by the Palestine and Babylonian schools. Of the two versions, the Babylonian Talmud Babli is regarded as the more complete and authoritative text and is studied much more frequently.

Literature

Cohen, Abraham. *Everyman's Talmud.* London: J. M. Dent & Sons, 1932. New York: Schocken, 1975.

Epstein, Isidore, ed. *The Babylonian Talmud.* 18 vols. London: Soncino, 1961.

Steinsaltz, Adin. *The Essential Talmud.* New York and London: Bantam, 1977.

Guhyasamaja Tantra

♦

The Assembly of Secrets, probably the earliest and most important of Buddhist Tantrik scriptures, is attributed to Asanga, the fourth-century *Yogacara master. This treatise, sometimes referred to as Samaja Tantra, or "the root *Tantra of all Tantras" was an instrumental text in the development of *Vajrayana. It belongs to the highest class of teachings: the

---

REALIA

קֶלָתָה Her basket. The source of this word is the Greek κάλαθος, *kalathos*, and it means a basket with a narrow base.

Illustration from a Greek drawing depicting such a basket of fruit.

CONCEPTS

פֵּאָה *Pe'ah*. One of the presents left for the poor (מַתְּנוֹת עֲנִיִּים). The Torah forbids harvesting "the corners of your field," so that the produce left standing may be harvested and kept by the poor (Leviticus 19:9). The Torah did not specify a minimum amount of produce to be left as *pe'ah*. But the Sages stipulated that it must be at least one sixtieth of the crop.

Pe'ah is set aside only from crops that ripen at one time and are harvested at one time. The poor are allowed to use their own initiative to reap the *pe'ah* left in the fields. But the owner of an orchard must see to it that each of the poor gets a fixed share of the *pe'ah* from places that are difficult to reach. The poor come to collect *pe'ah* three times a day. The laws of *pe'ah* are discussed in detail in tractate *Pe'ah*.

TRANSLATION AND COMMENTARY

[1]**and her husband threw her a bill of divorce into her lap or into her basket,** which she was carrying on her head, [2]**would you say here, too, that she would not** be divorced? Surely we know that the law is that she *is* divorced in such a case, as the Mishnah (*Gittin* 77a) states explicitly!

אָמַר לֵיהּ **Rav Ashi said** in reply to Ravina: The woman's **basket is considered to be at rest, and it is she who walks beneath it.** Thus the basket is considered to be a "stationary courtyard," and the woman acquires whatever is thrown into it.

MISHNAH הָיָה רוֹכֵב **If a per**son was riding on an animal **and he saw an ownerless object lying on the ground, and he said** to another person standing nearby, "Give that object to me," [5]**if the other person took the** ownerless object and said, "I **have acquired it for myself,"** he has acquired it by lifting it up, even though he was not the first to see it, and the rider has no claim to it. [7]But if, after he gave the object to the rider, the person who picked it up said, "I **acquired the object first."** [8]**he in fact said nothing.** His words are of no effect, and the rider may keep it. Since the person walking showed no intention of acquiring the object when he originally picked it up, he is not now believed when he claims that he acquired it first. Indeed, even if we maintain that when a person picks up an ownerless object on behalf of someone else, the latter does *not* acquire it automatically, here, by *giving* the object to the rider, he makes a gift of it to the rider.

GEMARA תְּנַן הָתָם [9]**We have learned elsewhere in a Mishnah in tractate** *Pe'ah* (4:9): "**Someone who gathered** *pe'ah.* — produce which by Torah law [Leviticus 23:22] is left unharvested in the corner of a field by the owner of the field, to be gleaned by the poor — **and said, 'Behold, this** *pe'ah* **which I have gleaned is intended for so-and-so the poor man;** [10]**Rabbi Eliezer says: The person who gathered the** *pe'ah* **has acquired it**

LITERAL TRANSLATION

in a public thoroughfare [1]**and [her husband] threw** in a bill of divorce into her lap or into her basket, [2]**here, too, would she not be divorced?**

[3]**He said to him: Her basket is at rest, and it is she who walks beneath it.**

MISHNAH [4][If a person] was riding on an animal and he saw a found object, and he said to another person, "Give it to me," [5][and the other person] took it and said, "I have acquired it," [6]**he has acquired it.** [7]If, after he gave it to him, he said, "I acquired it first," [8]**he said nothing.**

GEMARA [9]We have learned there: "Someone who gathered *pe'ah* and said, 'Behold this is for so-and-so the poor man,' [10]Rabbi Eliezer

---

בִּרְשׁוּת הָרַבִּים [1]וְזָרַק לָהּ גֵּט לְתוֹךְ חֵיקָהּ אוֹ לְתוֹךְ קַלָתָהּ — [2]הָכָא נַמֵי דְלָא מְגָרְשָׁה? [3]אָמַר לֵיהּ: קַלָתָהּ מֵינַח נָיְיחָא, וְאִיהִי דְּקָא מְסַגְּיָא מְתוּתַהּ.

מִשְׁנָה [4]הָיָה רוֹכֵב עַל גַּבֵּי בְהֶמָה וְרָאָה אֶת הַמְּצִיאָה, [5]וְאָמַר לַחֲבֵירוֹ "תְּנָה לִי", [5]נְטָלָהּ וְאָמַר, "אֲנִי זָכִיתִי בָהּ," [6]"זָכָה בָהּ. [7]אִם, מִשֶּׁנְּתָנָהּ לוֹ, אָמַר, "אֲנִי זָכִיתִי בָהּ תְּחִלָּה", [8]לֹא אָמַר כְּלוּם.

גְּמָרָא [9]תְּנַן הָתָם: "מִי שֶׁלִּקֵּט אֶת הַפֵּאָה וְאָמַר, "הֲרֵי זוֹ לִפְלוֹנִי עָנִי", [10]"רַבִּי אֱלִיעֶזֶר

RASHI

קלתה — סל שעל ראשה, שנותנת בה כלי מלאכתה ומזון שלה. הכי גמי דלא הוי ניחא — והלכן מען ממכבת גיטין (דף עז,א): זרק לה גיטה לתוך חיקה או לתוך קלתה — הרי זו מגורשת

משנה לא אמר כלום — דאפילו אמרינן המגביה מציאה מליחא לחבירו לא קנה חבירו, כיון דיהבה ליה — קנייה ממה נפשך. הי קניה קמא דלא מתכוין להקנות לחבירו — הא יהבה ניהליה ממתנה. ואי קניה קמא משום דלא היה מתכוין לקנות — הא ליה הסקך עד דמטא לידיה דהאי, וקנייא הוא כמא דעקריה מידיה דקמא לסם קנייה.

גמרא מי שליקט את הפאה — אדם מעלמא שאינו בעל שדה. דלא בעל שדה — לא אמר רבי אליעזר זכה, דליהא למימר "מגו" דגמציעיה", דאפילו הוא עני מחזר הוא לגלמן פאה משאר שלו, מדאמר בשמעיה חולין (קלא,ג): "לא מלקט לפני" — להוריד פני על שלו.

NOTES

מִי שֶׁלִּקֵּט אֶת הַפֵּאָה **If a person gathered** *pe'ah*. According to *Rashi*, the Mishnah must be referring to someone other than the owner of the field. By Torah law the owner of a field is required to separate part of his field as *pe'ah*, even if he himself is poor, and he may not take the *pe'ah* for himself. Therefore the "since" (מִגּוֹ) argument

---

HALAKHAH

קֶלָתָה **A woman's basket.** "If a man throws a bill of divorce into a basket his wife is holding, she thereby acquires the bill of divorce and the divorce takes effect." (*Shulhan Arukh, Even HaEzer* 139:10.)

הַמְּלַקֵּט פֵּאָה עֲבוּר אַחֵר **A person who gathered** *pe'ah* **for someone else.** "If a poor person, who is himself entitled to collect *pe'ah*, gathered *pe'ah* for another poor person, and said, 'This *pe'ah* is for X, the poor person,' he acquires

the *pe'ah* on behalf of that other poor person. But if the person who collected the *peuh* was wealthy, he does not acquire the *pe'ah* on behalf of the poor person. He must give it instead to the first poor person who appears in the field," following the opinion of the Sages, as explained by Rabbi Yehoshua ben Levi. (*Rambam, Sefer Zeraim, Hilkhot Mattenot Aniyyim* 2:19.)

Talmud. A sample page of a contemporary Talmud, with both Hebrew and English text and commentary.

anuttarayoga, or *Inner Tantra. The general tone of this early text can be gathered from the following quote: "No one succeeds in attaining perfection by employing difficult and vexing operations; but perfection can be gained by satisfying all one's desires."

The Samaja Tantra speaks of the virtues inherent in desire and sensory enjoyment, in the well-being of body and mind, and of realizing the Buddha nature through the union of female and male. The ancient text also states that if *siddhis*—that is, psychic powers—are to be acquired, women must be associated with those who attempt to reach this goal.

Passages of this Tantra—sometimes also called Tathagata Guhyaka—furthermore often demonstrate how *Tantra, even in a Buddhist setting, preserved its radical element of civil disobedience. This is also evident in other works such as the Prajnopaya-viniskaya Siddhi.

Literature
Wayman, Alex. *Yoga of the Guyasamaja Tantra: The Arcane Lore of Forty Verses.* Delhi: Motilal Banarsidass, 1977.

Mahayana-samparigraha
♦

This text is by Asanga (fourth century), the main founder of the *Yogacara school and the author to whom the Guhyasamaja Tantra has also been attributed. The work's title, Compendium of Mahayana, is misleading, since the text mainly expounds the basic teachings and philosophy of the Yogacara school only, which differ in many points from the other large school of early *Mahayana, the Madhyamaka school.

Avatamsaka Sutra
♦

This is the often-used short title for what is the Buddhavatamsaka Sutra, or the Sutra of the Garland of Buddhas. The text is one of the important *Vaipulya *sutras* of *Mahayana, and it embodies the sermons given by the historical Buddha after he had reached enlightenment as well as sayings attributed to the Buddhas of other, more heavenly realities.

Originally associated with the *Yogacara school, this *sutra* came to be the root text of the Chinese Hua-yen (Jap., Kegon) school of Mahayana Buddhism, but it is also generally respected by adherents of *Ch'an or *Zen. The text mainly teaches the unity and sameness of all phenomena, be they universe, mind, Buddhahood, or various types of sentient beings. Dating the original *Sanskrit text is difficult, since the only surviving manuscript is a fifth-century Chinese translation. In Japan, the work is known as Kegon Sutra.

Literature

Chang, Garma C. C., trans. *The Buddhist Teaching of Totality: The Philosophy of Hwa Yen Buddhism*. University Park, Pa., and London: Pennsylvania State University Press, 1971.

Cleary, Thomas, trans. *The Flower Ornament Scripture*. 3 vols. Boston and London: Shambhala, 1984–1987.

Denkart

♦

This encyclopedic work on religious lore was written in *Pahlavi, the language of southern Persia, in the late seventh century. In terms of concepts and beliefs, the contents here actually date back to the third or fourth centuries, when Zoroastrianism, the religion that brought forth the Avesta, had become an official state religion.

See also **Bundahishn.**

Literature

West, Edward William, ed. and trans. *Denkard: Books 5 and 7* and *Denkard: Books 8 and 9*. Sacred Books of the East series, Max Müller, ed., vol. 47. Oxford: Clarendon Press, 1882. Reprint. Delhi: Motilal Banarsidass, 1965. New York: Krishna, 1974.

Puranas

♦

This is the collective name (Skt., "old history") for a category of Indian sacred scriptures available not only to the priestly class of the Brahmins, as were the **Vedas,** but to the common people as well. Most of the Puranas were composed during or after the fourth century, but they often contain more ancient, devotional legends and traditions that reveal the beliefs and practices of early folk religion and popular *Hinduism. Of all these works, the Shiva Purana is one of the oldest, and portions of this text have been dated to before the common era.

Traditionally, there are eighteen principal Puranas (Skt., *maha-puranas*) and an unspecified number of minor ones. The texts were generally subdivided into three classes, according to the particular deity of the Hindu trinity they exalt most:

1. Brahma: for example, the Bhavishya and Brahmanda Puranas.
2. Vishnu: for example, the Vishnu and Bhagavata Puranas.
3. Shiva: for example, the Shiva Purana and the Agni Purana (also known as Vaju Purana).

Of special interest are the Markandeya Purana, a fifth- or sixth-century text that includes the **Devi Mahatmya,** and the eleventh-century Brahmanda Purana, which includes the **Lalita Sahasranama.** The eighteen major texts mainly exalt the three major male gods; of the so-called minor Puranas, however, a number are dedicated to some of the major goddesses of India— for example, the **Devi Purana** (sixth century) and the **Kalika Purana** (tenth century).

Literature

Pargiter, F. E., ed. and trans. *Markandeya Purana*. Calcutta: Asiatic Society of Bengal, 1904. Reprint 1969.

Wilson, Horace Hayman, trans. *Puranas: An Account of Their Contents and Nature*. Calcutta: Society for Indian Literature, 1911.

Midrash

◆

This term denotes a great number of texts, written between the fourth and fourteenth centuries, that draw on the originally oral tradition of the Jewish people. They constitute a verse-by-verse interpretation of the Hebrew scriptures, including legends, biblical exegesis, sermons, proverbs, commentaries, and ethical teachings. The individual Midrashim were written by diverse Jewish rabbis and teachers.

The Midrash Rabba, the major Midrash, is regarded as the most authoritative commentary on the Five Books of the Law of Moses (Torah/Pentateuch) and the so-called Five Scrolls (Ecclesiastes, Esther, Lamentations, Ruth, Song of Songs) of the Old Testament.

Literature
Brownlee, William H. *The Midrash Pesher of Habakkuk.* Missoula, Mont.: Scholars Press, 1977.

Abhidharmakosha

◆

The Treasure Chamber of the Abhidharma (see **Tripitaka**) was composed by Vasubandhu (c. 400 C.E.) of Kashmir, an adept of both the Sarvastivada (*Hinayana) and Yogacara (*Mahayana) schools. It consists of six hundred verses (Abhidharmakosha-karika) and a commentary (Abhidharmakosha-bhashya) on these. The fifth-century text was the most influential and authoritative compilation of Sarvastivada teachings and is especially interesting in that it reflects the transition from Hinayana to Mahayana *Buddhism.

The Abhidharmakosha is extant in Chinese and Tibetan translations and has been very influential in the development of Buddhism in China. It is also part of the Chinese collection of Buddhist texts known as **San-tsang.**

The work is known in Japan as Kusharon.

Devi Mahatmya

♦

This work is the first large and comprehensive text in *Sanskrit literature that specifically deals with the Indian tradition of the Great Goddess (Skt., *devi*). Although this Glorification of the Great Goddess was certainly influenced by Vedic *Brahmanism, in itself it is a major scripture of *Shakta, then apparently evolving and attempting to reestablish the position the goddess had held in pre-Aryan, pre-Vedic times.

The Devi Mahatmya, actually a part of the Markandeya **Purana** but clearly having independent status, reminds us that the ultimate reality of the most ancient human traditions has always been recognized as female and venerated in the form of a goddess.

The Devi is shown here in her manifold aspects, among which are the archetypal virgin (Kanya, Kumari) and mother (Ambika) and the wanton (Kamakhya) and virtuous woman (Sati), demonstrating that apparent dualities are in fact merely possibilities of manifestation.

Literature
Coburn, Thomas B. *Devi Mahatmya*. Delhi: Motilal Banarsidass, 1984.
Pargiter, F. E., trans. *Markandeya Purana*. Calcutta: Asiatic Society of Bengal, 1904. Reprint 1969.

Third Shelf
500 C.E.–1000 C.E.

Samhitas
Kubjika Tantra
Mahacinacara-sara Tantra
Devi Purana
Bundahishn
Hsin-hsin-ming
Qur'an
Prajnopaya-viniscaya Siddhi
San-tsang
Ginza
Hadith
Kalachakra Tantra
Mabinogion
Edda
Vajra Songs
T'an-ching

The Life and Liberation of Padmasambhava
Hevajra Tantra
Bardo Thödol
Dharanis
Teachings of the Golden Flower of the Supreme One
The Secret Life and Songs of Lady Yeshe Tsogyal
Sepher Yetsirah
Kobo Daishi Zenshu
San-mei k'o
Kumari Tantra
Kalika Purana
Kalivilasa Tantra
Engisiki (or Engishiki)
Yamalas
Agamas

Samhitas

◆

In its most specific sense, the term *samhita* (Skt., "collection") is the title for the most ancient collections of hymns that make up the Vedas, texts upon which the **Aranyakas, Brahmanas,** and **Upanishads** follow.

Today, however, the term is mainly used to indicate a collection of roughly two hundred scriptures of the *Vaishnava school. Influences from *Tantra and *Shakta are apparent in texts such as the Nisvasa-Tattva Samhita and the Jayakhya Samhita, which originated in the fifth century and are scriptures belonging to Hindu Tantra. Two of the more widely known Samhitas are the Gheranda Samhita and Shiva Samhita, both dating from the late seventeenth century; the latter is obviously not Vaishnava but *Shaiva oriented.

Kubjika Tantra

◆

This sixth-century text of seventeen chapters, also known as Kubjika-mata, is of *Kula origin. The Kubjika Tantra, like the **Mahacinacara-sara Tantra,** is a scripture that raises the question of whether or not *Tantra has been influenced by the import of techniques from Chinese *Taoism. Chapter 16, for example, describes a certain mode of worship stated to be derived from Mahacina, the ancient Indian name for China.

Chapter 16 describes three specific and "effective means" of achieving rare success. One of these suggests that a girl of sixteen should be worshiped by visual, focused meditation on every part of her body; the meditation should be accomplished while repeating chants and prayers and without being influenced by passion.

Mahacinacara-sara Tantra

◆

A short *Tantra of only six chapters, which speaks of the many travels and

118

spiritual experiences of a man called Vasistha, this work seems designed to combine orthodox Buddhist teachings with those of Chinese *Taoism and/or Indian *Tantra. After having worshiped the goddess Tara and visited the sacred ground of *Kamakhya in Assam, the main character finally goes to China (Skt., Mahacina), where he encounters the Buddha. In Chapter 2 he finds the famous founder of *Buddhism "contrary to the nature of a person like him" seated in a rather erotic environment, "surrounded by a thousand damsels and drunk" (S. C. Banerjee, 1988, p. 237). He is told, however, that this *cinacara* is proper for one who worships the goddess. The Buddha also explains that mental worship and the worship of women are the best forms one can practice.

Devi Purana

◆

One of the Puranas of the *Shakta school, written in Bengal at some time during the sixth century. It is dedicated to Devi, a *Sanskrit general term meaning "goddess" and often used as a synonym for *Shakti and/or as a title for other goddesses. Like the slightly earlier **Devi Mahatmya**, the Devi Purana makes obvious references to a pre-Vedic worship of the goddess in India and declares the worship of her open to members of all castes. The text is only available in Bengali with Hindi commentaries.

Bundahishn

◆

In Zoroastrianism, *bundahishn* is the term used to indicate the process of creation. It is also the popular name of a Persian text, written in *Pahlavi and with an alternative name of Zand-Agahih, that explains the origins, nature, and purpose of divine creation. Essentially, the text represents a compilation of ancient teachings on cosmology that are also contained in the **Avesta,** but which here are written for the noble laymen rather than for clerical use; only nobles, of course, were literate among laypeople.

Preserved copies of the Bundahishn have been dated to the tenth century, but its origins can be traced back to the period between the fourth and seventh centuries.

Hsin-hsin-ming

♦

Much more well known under the Japanese title Shinjinmei, the Chinese Hsin-hsin-ming was written in 595 by the master Seng-ts'an (c. 550–606), himself better known by his Japanese names of Sosan or Tozan.

The text is one of the very early documents of *Ch'an Buddhism, of which Seng-ts'an is the third patriarch. This poetic work shows strong traces of *Taoism, and as such, it is an important document testifying to the emerging teachings that combined traditions of Indian *Mahayana Buddhism with Chinese Taoism, thus creating Ch'an and, ultimately, Japanese *Zen Buddhism.

See also the quote at the beginning of this book.

Literature
Blyth, Reginald Horace. *Zen and Zen Classics*. 5 vols. Tokyo: Hokuseido Press, 1960–1970.

Qur'an

♦

This is the sacred book of Islam, containing the 114 *suras,* or chapters, said by believers to have been divinely revealed from the year 610 onwards by Allah to Muhammad. The Arabic name of the book translates as "The Recital," referring to the angel Gabriel's order to Muhammad: "Recite!"

The Qur'an, as we know it, teaches a pure monotheism with an absolute obeisance to its One God, Allah, and the text is virtual law to the faithful believer. The work, also often spelled as Koran, consists of legal, ethical, theological, and sociological rules and guidelines along with mythical and prophetic material; the final edition and canonization of the text is tradi-

Qur'an. Title page of a fourteenth century manuscript of the Qur'an in the Vice-regal Library of Cairo.

tionally ascribed to the time between the years 644 and 656 (a dating that is sometimes challenged as being too early).

The text accuses both Judaism and Christianity of having disobeyed and falsified the divine precepts of the great patriarchal god, and it attempts to lead humanity back toward what is conceived as the right way. A radical yet persuasive theory holds, however, that at the root of the holy Qur'an is perhaps the "Word of Qure," the wisdom of the pre-Islamic Arabian triple goddess of the moon as it was written down by her priestesses, which only later was transformed into the book of law and order that was allegedly received by the prophet. Barbara Walker, in her book *The Woman's Encyclopedia of Myths and Secrets,* suggests: "Worshippers of Kore or Q're were the original authors of the oldest section of the Koran. Even Muslims admit this work existed many centuries before the time of Muhammad. Legend said it was copied from a divine prototype that appeared in heaven at the beginning of eternity, the Preserved Tablet, or Mother of the Book" (1983, p. 55).

Literature

Dawood, N. J., trans. *The Koran.* Harmondsworth, England: Penguin Books, 1956; 4th ed., rev., 1974.

Gatje, H. *The Qur'an and Its Exegesis: Selected Texts.* Berkeley, Calif.: University of California Press, 1976.

Jeffery, Arthur. *The Qur'an As Scripture.* New York: R. F. Moore, 1952. Reprint. New York: Arno, 1980.

Prajnopaya-viniscaya Siddhi

♦

This is one of the early Buddhist Tantras, originating in the late seventh or early eighth century. Attributed to Anangavajra, one of the eighty-four *Mahasiddhas, the work contains a number of features that highlight the earliest *Vajrayana teachings at the time that both *Tantra and *Buddhism made their entry into Tibet, a few centuries after *Shakta and Tantra had come into prominence in areas such as Assam and Bengal.

The work describes a number of *siddhis* (extrasensory or paranormal skills), advocates sexuality as a spiritual technique, and even allows sexual union between mother and son, brother and sister, or father and daughter. The work also clearly defines *prajna,* the "perfection of wisdom," as a female prerogative—as something that can be obtained by men only through the agency of women.

San-tsang

◆

Sometimes also designated as **Tripitaka,** but not to be confused with that Indian collection of Buddhist texts, the San-tsang represents a major body of Chinese translations of scriptures imported from India. The collection is named after its translator, Hsüan-tsang (600–664), a Chinese monk who spent sixteen years in India and brought back important Buddhist texts.

The texts in the San-tsang collection vary as to their background; it includes Hinayana works translated from *Pali and Mahayana texts translated from *Sanskrit. To these, the collection adds original Chinese Buddhist texts and, of course, specifically Chinese commentaries on these teachings. Some of the more important works in this collection are the Prajnaparamita Sutra and the Abhidharmakosha.

Ginza

◆

The Ginza, or "treasure," is the major scripture of the *Mandaeans, a Gnostic school whose teachings comprise a syncretic religion influenced by many sources. The text, dated to about the year 700, describes the creation of the world, speaks of the soul's existence after death, and generally repudiates most teachings of the Jewish scriptures. The Ginza is also a general suppository of magical lore and cosmological speculation, reflecting the religious and moral concepts of the school and its members.

The Mandaean teachings, part of the religious movement called

*Gnosticism, speak out against circumcision and celibacy, encourage marriage and childbearing, and, in general, sketch human life as a constant struggle against evil and darkness.

Hadith

♦

The Hadith "stories" constitute a large body of Islamic traditions and are an important source for Islamic law (*sunna*). The Hadith are not part of the Qur'an but are regarded as second in importance only to that sacred text.

These collections of texts include the sayings of the prophet Muhammad (c. 570–632) and his companions, as well as texts by later prominent Islamic thinkers. The number of Hadith had grown to extreme proportions by the ninth century—one source says they numbered six hundred thousand—and scholars and lawyers were charged with critically evaluating and reducing the number of texts. Canonical recognition was finally given, in the ninth century, to six collections of four thousand Hadith each. The two most reliable and credible collections, after all the texts had been categorized into degrees of authenticity, became known as the two Sahihs, or "sound collections."

Literature
Ali, Muhammad. *A Manual of Hadith*. Atlantic Highlands, N.J.: Humanities Press, 1978.
Guillaume, Alfred. *The Traditions of Islam: An Introduction to the Study of Hadith Literature*. Oxford: Clarendon Press, 1924. Reprint. New York: Books for Libraries, 1980.

Kalachakra Tantra

♦

This Buddhist *Tantra was introduced to Tibet in the tenth century. The text describes the function of the *nadi* (the subtle channels of energy within

Kalachakra Tantra. A typical traditional image of the Vajrayogini, a goddess who plays an important role in many Tantrik visualizations and initiations and who appears in many of the Tibetan ★Tantras.

the body), teaches six types of meditation practice, and deals with such sciences as astronomy, geography, and psychology. The scripture has been especially valued by the Jonangpa school of *Vajrayana, but it is taught in other schools as well.

The Kalachakra Tantra and its associated rituals laid the basis for the Tibetan calendar, which started in 946, and is said to have originated in India at least three hundred years before it reached Tibet. The work also contains some of the teachings that later became known as the Six Doctrines of Naropa, or **Naro Chos-drug.**

Mabinogion
♦

This medieval collection of legends originating in Wales was originally found in two different manuscripts and later compiled into one work. The stories of this Mabinogi cycle are based on the White Book of Rhydderch, written between 1300 and 1325, and the Red Book of Hergest, the author of which lived between 1375 and 1425. Although the manuscripts are thus from the fourteenth and perhaps the fifteenth century, the legends themselves are much older and are clearly derived from the Celtic tradition. There is as yet no definitive evidence for dating this material; the period between the seventh and ninth centuries is the most likely.

The Mabinogion's myths and tales have much in common with Irish traditions, and the work also contains three romances that belong to the legends surrounding King Arthur.

Literature
Jones, G., and T. Jones, trans. *The Mabinogion.* New York: Dutton, 1949.

Edda
♦

The title Edda is used for two different works that allow insights into the mythology and legends of northern European peoples of more than a

Edda. A page from the Verse Edda, from a manuscript known as Codex Regius. The page recounts the so-called Doom of the Gods and belongs to the Voluspa section.

thousand years ago. Both texts were originally written in the language of Iceland, yet they are distinctly different in style and content. Although the actual writing of the Verse Edda and the Prose Edda, sometimes translated as "Tales of the Grandmother," took place in the ninth and the thirteenth centuries, respectively, one must assume that the traditions date from at least two or three hundred years earlier.

The Poetic, or Verse, Edda represents a compilation of thirty-four to thirty-seven poems or hymns that represent orally transmitted myths of Germanic peoples, Vikings and other northern Europeans, put into writing at some time between the years 800 and 900. Most of the text is extant in the so-called Codex Regius, although most editions of the Edda also include other material. This Verse Edda contains such famous legends and songs as the Voluspa, Volsunga, and Nibelung sagas. In fact, most of what is known of the old northern deities such as Freya or Balder, Thor and Odin, apart from the hostile and ill-informed Roman accounts, stems from this source, which also speaks of the symbolism involved in the runic alphabet.

The Younger, or Prose, Edda, on the other hand, is a medieval collection of more specifically Norse myths that was written and compiled by the Icelandic chieftain Snorri Sturluson (1179–1241) in 1220. Sturluson does frequently quote from the earlier Edda, but his text, we must remind ourselves, was compiled about two hundred years after the introduction of Christianity. The ancient traditions were already becoming suspect and suppressed, and his prologue, for example, includes clear references to the Bible.

Literature

Hollander, Lee Milton, trans. *The Poetic Edda*. Austin, Tex.: University of Texas Press, 1962. Reprint 1964.

Young, Jean Isobel, trans. *The Prose Edda of Snorri Sturluson.* Berkeley, Calif.: University of California Press, 1964.

Vajra Songs

♦

These songs and poems were written by a number of Tantrik adepts and teachers in order to provide "teaching stories" that could easily be learned

*Vajra Songs. The *Mahasiddha Savaripa and his wife/lover. The proud and professional hunter learned to abstain from killing and to use his skills in order to attain enlightenment with "the arrow of ultimate truth."*

by heart and transmitted orally. The tradition started with the *Mahasiddhas of old and continued with adepts of the *Kagyud-pa lineage through the ages and up to the present day.

The Legends of the Eighty-four Mahasiddhas, for example, are Tibetan manuscripts that describe, in song and prose, the lives and spiritual adventures of the renowned Indian Tantriks who lived and taught during the seventh through tenth centuries. These Mahasiddhas were instrumental in the development of Tibetan *Buddhism. Among this group of revered masters, some of whom were fishermen, kings, thieves, or princesses, we find such illuminated figures as Naropa (1016–1100), Saraha (c. 780), and Tilopa (988–1069), whose lifestyle and teachings influenced even more famous masters as, for example, Milarepa (c. 1039–1123), well known for his Hundred Thousand Songs (see **Mila Gnubum**).

Similar to the songs of these masters—which, for centuries, have kept that tradition alive, first orally and then in written form—are the Vajra Songs of lamas belonging to the Kagyud-pa school of *Vajrayana; this collection of texts is known as the Kagyu Gurtso. According to Chögyam Trungpa (1940–1987), an incarnated master of that tradition, these songs represent "the best of the butter which has been churned from the ocean of milk of the Buddha's teachings" (1980, p. xiii). The Kagyu Gurtso, published as recently as 1980 under the title *Rain of Wisdom,* includes texts composed by masters of Tibetan *Tantra spanning one thousand years from the early tenth century through to the late twentieth century.

Literature

Dowman, Keith, trans. *Masters of Mahamudra: Songs and Histories of the Eighty-Four Buddhist Siddhas.* New York: State University of New York Press, 1985.

———. *Masters of Enchantment: The Lives and Legends of the Mahasiddhas.* Rochester, Vt.: Inner Traditions International, 1988.

Robinson, James B., trans. *Buddha's Lions: The Lives of the Eighty-Four Siddhas.* Berkeley, Calif.: Dharma Publishing, 1979.

Trungpa, Chögyam, and the Nalanda Translation Committee. *The Rain of Wisdom: The Vajra Songs of the Kagy Gurus.* Boston and London: Shambhala, 1980.

T'an-ching

◆

Popularly known as Platform Sutra or Sutra of Hui-neng, the full title of this Chinese text is Liu-tsu-ta-shih fa-pao-t'an-ching, or The Sutra of the Sixth Patriarch Spoken from the High Seat. The text contains the biography and discourses of Hui-neng (638–713), also known as Wei-lang (or by his Japanese name, E'no), who has become famous for this most profound and enlightened text of *Ch'an and *Zen literature.

Hui-neng is the sixth patriarch of Ch'an *Buddhism and is often seen as the person who actually made Ch'an into a truly Chinese school, a school that before him had still been steeped in Indian traditions.

Literature

Chan, Wing Tsit, trans. *The Platform Scripture*. New York: St. John's University Press, 1963.

Hui Neng. *The Sixth Patriarch's Dharma Jewel Platform Sutra*. San Francisco, Calif.: Buddhist Text Translation Society, 1977.

Price, A. F., trans., and Mou-lam Wong. *The Diamond Sutra and the Sutra of Hui Neng*. Boston: Shambhala, 1969. Reprint 1985.

The Life and Liberation of Padmasambhava

◆

According to tradition, this is a *terma* discovered by the *terton* Urgyan Lingpa (b. 1323). This biographical *terma* is also known as *Sheldrakma*, a short transliteration of the complete Tibetan title Padma bKa'-thang Shel-brag-ma. The text represents the story of Padmasambhava (717–804), the yogi and magician who is often credited with bringing *Buddhism to Tibet and thus being the founder of *Vajrayana.

Traditionally, the text is regarded as the official biography of the great adept, a work that was written by his lover and student, Lady Yeshe Tsogyal (757–817). It is a beautiful, poetic work that allows the reader to form a rather intimate picture of the main characters and also of life and religion in Tibet: the coming of Buddhism and its initial struggle with the indigenous *Bön religion.

The text is especially valued among members of the *Nyingma-pa school and the practitioners of *Dzogchen.

Literature
Tsogyal, Yeshe. *The Life and Liberation of Padmasambhava*. 2 vols. Berkeley, Calif.: Dharma Publications, 1978.

Hevajra Tantra

♦

This Buddhist *Tantra of twenty chapters is believed to have originated in the early eighth century. The deity Hevajra is a personified symbol for the Buddhist concept of a supreme being in a state of nonduality; Hevajra is most often imagined or shown in the position known as *yab-yum,* a mutual embrace between male and female.

The Tantra teaches, among other things, the "Union of Skillful Means (male) and Profound Cognition (female)" and states that sexual union can be helpful in achieving the psychic powers known as *siddhis. The text belongs to the higher or *Inner Tantras and includes the famous Tantrik quote that explains a major tenet of *Tantra in only a few words: "One must rise by that by which one falls."

Literature
Snellgrove, David L. *Hevajra Tantra: A Critical Study*. 2 vols. London: Oxford University Press, 1959. Reprint 1980.

Bardo Thödol

♦

Western translators and publishers call this text The Tibetan Book of the Dead, a translation that seems misguiding to the less-informed reader. A better translation would be "Liberation by Hearing during one's Existence in the Bardo." True, the Tibetan term *bardo* is used to indicate the intermediate phase through which one must pass, according to these teachings,

Bardo Thödol. Two folios (35a and 67a) from a Tibetan edition of the text. The central mandalas are in color and show the peaceful (upper folio) and wrathful deities encountered in the bardo.

between death and one's next rebirth or reincarnation. Nonetheless, *bardo* ("in-between state") also stands for other states of mind, not all of which are connected with death. These states are differentiated as follows:

1. the *bardo* of birth
2. the dream *bardo*
3. the *bardo* resulting from meditation
4. the *bardo* of the moment of death
5. the *bardo* of supreme reality
6. the *bardo* of becoming

Only the last three states (4–6) are part of the period during which an individual is believed to remain in a kind of limbo between death and birth, a period that lasts forty-nine days. The text is read aloud (liberation by hearing) to someone in *bardo,* sometimes as pure instruction for meditation and, at the time of death, to prepare the mind for the adventures ahead.

The text itself is based on the oral teachings of Padmasambhava; it was first composed around 760 and was rediscovered (see *terma) and extended in the fourteenth century. It has also been strongly influenced by Tibet's most indigenous religion, *Bön, and shows clear traces of this shamanic system of beliefs, of original Tibetan psychology, and ingenious divinities. See also **Naro Chos-drug.**

Literature
Evans-Wentz, W. Y. *The Tibetan Book of the Dead.* New York: Oxford University Press, 1927. Reprint 1960.

Freemantle, Francesca, and Chögyam Trungpa. *The Tibetan Book of the Dead: The Great Liberation Through Hearing in the Bardo.* Boston and London: Shambhala, 1975.

Lauf, Detlef Ingo. *Secret Doctrines of the Tibetan Books of the Dead.* Boston and London: Shambhala, 1977.

Dharanis

♦

Dharani (from Skt., dharana, "concentration") is the name for a genre of short *sutras concerned with a specific magical formula, similar to a mantra but much longer. Such texts play a significant role in Tantrik *Buddhism, for example, in the Tibetan *Vajrayana, Chinese *Mi-tsung, and Japanese *Shingon schools, movements that were all founded during the eighth and ninth centuries.

The Dharanis constitute texts designed to convey the secret, essential contents of a teaching. This is achieved by a recital of the symbol-laden syllables, thus sensitizing the worshiper and leading her or him into a particular state of mind.

Teachings of the Golden Flower
of the Supreme One

♦

The teachings concerning the Secret of the Golden Flower seem to have originated with the Taoist Dragon Gate school (Chin., Lung-men), an offshoot of the better-known Way of the Realization of Truth (Chin., Ch'üan-chen Tao), a school that combined the teachings of religious *Taoism with certain concepts of Buddhist and even Confucian origin. The oral roots of the teachings presented here go back to at least the eighth century, and in printed form the work can be traced back to the seventeenth century, with probably an intermediate period of handwritten texts circulated among a small number of initiates only.

The Golden Flower, a term that refers to the Taoist concept of an immortal spirit body, can be awakened, according to the text, by a number of psychophysical exercises and techniques that aim at a controlled use of the life energies and are designed to lead the practitioner toward a complete integration of his or her personality.

Unfortunately, the available manuscripts of this work—in Chinese known as T'ai-i chin-hua tsung-chih—are incomplete. Later editions of the available German and English translations therefore include portions of another, similar text with the title Hui-ming Ching, "The Book of Consciousness and Life."

Literature

Wilhelm, Richard, trans. *The Secret of the Golden Flower: A Chinese Book of Life.* New, rev., and augm. ed., translated into English by C. F. Baynes. New York: Harcourt, Brace & Jovanovich, 1962.

The Secret Life and Songs
of Lady Yeshe Tsogyal

♦

An eighteenth-century *terma* revealed by the *terton* Taksham Nuden Dorje, this text represents a biography of Yeshe Tsogyal (757–817), one of the few women important to the spread of *Buddhism in Tibet. The work recounts her adventurous life as student and lover of Padmasambhava (see **The Life and Liberation of Padmasambhava**), relates the events and effects of her initiations, and is a general account of her efforts to spread the early teachings of *Vajrayana, especially the traditions that are represented by the *Dzogchen and *Nyingma schools.

Literature
Dowman, Keith, trans. *Sky Dancer: The Secret Life and Songs of the Lady Yeshe Tsogyel.* London: Routledge & Kegan Paul, 1984.
Tulku, Tarthang, trans. *Mother of Knowledge: The Enlightenment of Yeshes mTsho-rgyal.* Berkeley, Calif.: Dharma Publishing, 1983.

Sepher Yetsirah

◆

This ninth-century Book of Formation, also spelled Sepher Yetzirah or Sefer Yesirah, is one of the four most important works of cabalistic literature. In speaking of the cabalistic Tree of Life, its paths and the associated letters of the Hebrew alphabet, the work essentially explains, in its six chapters, the structure of the universe and the flow of energies within it.

Although the text has often been regarded as belonging to Judaic mysticism, more recent interpretation, especially that offered by Carlo Suares, indicates that it actually represents a tradition of independent, non-Mosaic initiates.

See also **Genesis, Song of Songs, Sepher ha Zohar.**

Literature
Suares, Carlo. *The Sepher Yetsirah: Including the Original Astrology According to Qabala and Its Zodiac.* Boulder and London: Shambhala, 1976.

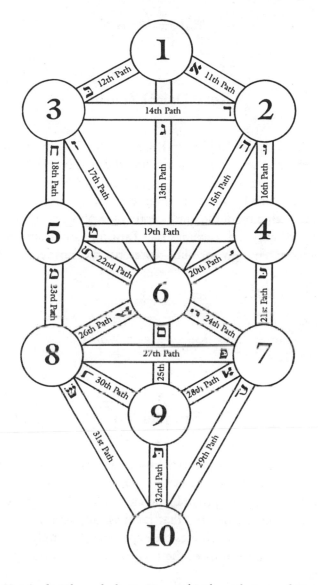

Sepher Yetsirah. The cabalistic Tree of Life with its traditional ten spheres and their twenty-two connecting pathways, each of which is assigned one of the twenty-two Hebrew glyphs. The hidden, or secret, eleventh sphere is located in the center of the square between positions two and five.

Kobo Daishi Zenshu

♦

This work is by Kobo Daishi, or Kukai (774–835), the founder of the Japanese *Shingon school of *Buddhism who had been trained and educated in the teachings of the *Mi-tsung school in China.

First written when he was only seventeen and finalized about a decade later—at the beginning of the ninth century—Kobo Daishi's text attempts to classify and unify the teachings of *Taoism, Confucianism, and Buddhism; Shingon, naturally for him, represents the most comprehensive of all these systems.

See also Dharanis.

Literature

Hakeda, Yoshito S., trans. *Kukai: Major Works*. New York: Columbia University Press, 1972.

San-mei-k'o

♦

Chinese in origin, yet today better known by its Japanese name Hokyo Zanmai, this *Ch'an Buddhist text dates from the ninth century and was written by the master Tung-shan Liang-chieh (807–869). The work mainly speaks of the "Buddha nature" that is intrisically present in all humans, even in all things, and it celebrates the experience of simply being who and what you are—in the words of the text, of the "suchness" of experience and existence.

The Chinese title itself translates as "The Song of the Treasure House of Mirrorlike Enlightenment."

Literature

Cleary, Thomas, trans. *Timeless Spring: A Soto Zen Anthology*. New York: Weatherhill, 1980.

*Kumari Tantra. A popular image of the Indian goddess *Kali, the dark Great Mother of Time, Life, and Death.*

Kumari Tantra

♦

This anonymous, but certainly *Kula-affiliated, work of nine chapters is notable mainly because it is one the few texts that openly speaks of human sacrifice, which at the time was still regarded as a sometimes-required ritual. The scripture calls for the blood of a human being, sheep, buffalo, cat, or mouse to be used in a mass dedicated to the goddess *Kali—and it states quite explicitly that human sacrifice is the best.

The Kumari Tantra recommends, among other things, worship of the goddess in a cemetery and describes the sacrifices to be made to Kali. Such worship is said to be even more beneficial than whatever ritual might be performed in one of the goddess's famous and sacred places of worship. Another integral part of worship, according to this text, is the recital of sacred chants while meditating before a naked Kula woman. The text has not been clearly dated and probably was composed between the ninth and twelfth centuries.

Kalika Purana

♦

This so-called minor **Purana** originated within the folds of *Shakta and *Tantra as it developed in Assam and Bengal—systems of belief in which the goddess is recognized as principal deity and source of universal energy. The text consists of nine thousand stanzas in ninety-eight chapters and has been dated to the tenth century. The work is concerned mainly with describing the worship of the goddess *Kali, or Kalika, and especially with the veneration of *Kamakhya, an erotic aspect of the Great Goddess Mahamaya.

The Kalika Purana is also known, and both feared and slandered, for its detailed description of human sacrifice, a not-uncommon ritual in ancient times. The work is sometimes known as Kalika Tantra.

Literature
Kooij, K. R. van. *Worship of the Goddess According to the Kalikapurana.* Leiden, Netherlands: Brill, 1972.

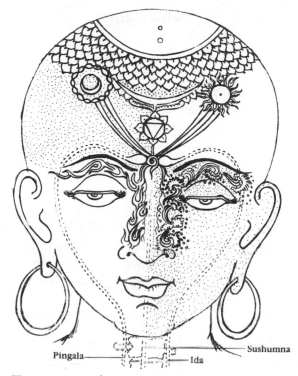

Kalivilasa Tantra. *According to Tantrik subtle physiology, currents of lunar (Ida) and solar (Pingala) energy cross the central channel (Sushumna) in the area of the third eye.*

Kalivilasa Tantra

♦

This East Indian work of unknown age contains, apart from the more-or-less usual topics found in such texts, some interesting information not found elsewhere or in such explicit language.

The text stresses the general importance of sexuality as the means to attain liberation and makes special allowance, in chapter 11, for union even with someone who is married to someone else. The Kalivilasa states that such union is allowed provided that both partners are initiates and the man is able to retain the discharge of semen. Rather than ejaculation, the scripture admonishes, the devotee should give an upward motion to the seed energy in order to make it reach the brain and the higher *chakras,* centers of subtle energy according to Tantrik and general Indian tradition.

Engisiki (or Engishiki)

♦

This title derives from the Engi era of Japanese history (901–922) and is a collective name for fifty books on the laws of early Japan, completed in 927. The religious laws are contained in the first ten of these books, most of which deal with Jingi-ryo, the laws concerning the ceremonies and rituals of *Shinto. Book 8 of the Engisiki contains most of the *norito,* the official prayers and liturgies.

Literature
Bock, F., trans. *Engi-shiki: Procedures of the Engi Era, 1549–1650.* Berkeley, Calif.: University of California Press, 1967. Reprint 1974.

Yamalas

♦

These texts represent a specific class of *Shakta scriptures, also called Yamala Tantras, most of which were composed during the tenth or eleventh centuries. In general, the texts are neither purely *Vamacara- or Dakshinacara-oriented; they seem to represent a developmental phase during which "left-handed" *Tantra was beginning to be replaced by the "right-handed" version.

As with the **Upanishads** and **Puranas,** there is a traditional classification of these texts into so-called principal and minor works. Both categories together number ninety-one, and each of the works bears the name of a particular god or goddess: for instance, Brahma Yamala, Ganesha Yamala, Lakshmi Yamala, Rudra Yamala, Skanda Yamala, Uma Yamala, and Vishnu Yamala.

The *Sanskrit term *yamala* not only refers to this group of scriptures, but also means "couple" or "pair" and is used to indicate a painting or sculpture showing a male and female deity in sexual union; the same position is known as *yab-yum* in Tibet and as *sambara* in Nepal.

Agamas

♦

In *Hinduism, the Agamas (Skt., "Source of the Teaching") constitute a class of scriptures that mainly contain *Shaiva teachings concerning ritual and cosmology. They are written in the form of supposed dialogues between the goddess *Parvati (or *Shakti) and the god *Shiva, and they mark the appearance of *Shakta influence among the Shaiva groups in Tamil Nadu, a south Indian province. Among the approximately two hundred texts, twenty-eight are regarded as the Shaiva equivalent to the northern Vedas and, like the Mahabharata, they are sometimes called the "Fifth Veda." These texts have not yet been studied or researched in detail.

In *Buddhism the term Agamas is used as a synonym for the *Pali *nikayas* and indicates the *Mahayana versions of the texts that constitute the Sutra Pitaka (see Tripitaka). These four Agamas are known under the following names: Dirghagama, Madhyamagama, Samyuktagama, and Ekottaragama (or Ekottarikagama).

Literature
Smith, David H. *The Smith Agama Collection: Sanskrit Books and Manuscripts Relating to the Pancaratra Studies*. Syracuse: Syracuse University Press, 1978.

Fourth Shelf
1000 C.E.–1850 C.E.

Ganeshgita
Tonalpohualli
Kularnava Tantra
Abhidhammattha-sangaha
Naro Chos-drug
Lalita Sahasranama
Ching-te ch'uan-teng-lu
Nila Tantra
Mila Gnubum and Mila Khabum
Jewel Ornament of Liberation
Li-chiao shih wu-lun
Tannisho
Niruttara Tantra
Pi Yän Lu
Sepher ha Zohar
Kanjur

Kaulavali Nirnaya Tantra
The Ten Pictures of the Ox
Shobo genzo
Wu-men-kuan
Yoga Upanishads
Yogini Tantra
Yoni Tantra
Gheranda Samhita
Shiva Samhita
Adi Granth
Mahanirvana Tantra
Walam Olum
The Book of Mormon
Kitab-i-Iqan
Kalevala

Ganeshgita

♦

This is the name given for a curious version of the **Bhagavadgita** that has been prepared and used by the Ganapatyas, a small sect venerating the elephant-headed god Ganesha, a deity of fortune, prosperity, and health. In this Gita, created almost a thousand years after its classical predecessor, every occurrence of the name of Krishna has simply been replaced by that of Ganesha, apart from which the books are virtually identical.

Tonalpohualli

♦

Tonalpohualli are the ritual and divinatory texts of Mesoamerican cultures. The term is usually translated as "sacred almanacs" and is thus a fitting title for the various pieces of the Mayan, Mixtec, and Aztec written traditions that survived the destructive zeal of the Spanish Christian invaders.

The few extant texts, such as Codex Borgia, Codex Madrid, and Codex Vaticanus B, were written in hieroglyphic pictures meant to be read and interpreted by specialists trained in the oral traditions; the texts essentially served as mnemonic aids. More parts of the large body of myths and traditions that must once have existed have also been found as vase paintings; such art depicts the adventures and deeds of gods and goddesses and many a myth which, in oral form, is still known among the modern descendents of the ancient cultures.

A number of Mayan pictorial texts, if one may call them texts, were concerned with that society's precise keeping of time and were chiseled into the walls of temples and palaces. A well-known example of such work is the so-called Calendar Stone.

Similar, yet less spiritually and rather historically oriented codices are known as Codex Bodley and Codex Columbino. These texts mainly contain genealogical records concerning the succession of dynasties and rulers. This pictographic tradition continued for some time after the

Tonalpohualli. *An example of extraordinary Mayan art found at the ceremonial center at Yaxchilan (Menche). This seventh-century stonecarving has been variously interpreted as a sacrificial scene or as a penitent kneeling before a priest and inflicting punishment on himself.*

Spanish Conquest. One still-existing Aztec manual, now known as the Codex Mendoza, recounts life at Tenochtitlan, the famous Aztec capital.

See also **Pop Wuj.**

Literature
Thompson, John Eric Sidney. *Maya History and Religion.* Norman, Okla.: University of Oklahoma Press, 1970.
————. *Maya Hieroglyphic Writing: An Introduction.* 3rd ed., rev. Norman, Okla.: University of Oklahoma Press, 1966.

Kularnava Tantra

♦

Perhaps the foremost theoretical and philosophical *Tantra of the *Kula school, this text consists of two thousand verses in seventeen chapters and was probably written during the period of the tenth through the twelfth centuries. The work is set up as a series of questions by *Shakti that are answered by *Shiva.

The Kularnava Tantra is much concerned with establishing "proof" that Kula teachings are the most valid; it also warns of false teachers, explains the doctrine's relevant terminology and concepts, and lays down its rules and regulations. According to this text, Kula knowledge can be gained "by one who has pure mind, and whose senses are controlled." In Chapter 2 the Tantra warns that the "Kula path is frought with danger. In fact, it is more difficult than walking on a sword-edge, clinging to a tiger's neck and holding a serpent."

Literature
Woodroffe, Sir John, and Madhav Pundalik Pandit. *Kularnava Tantra.* Madras: Ganesh & Co., 1974.

*Kularnava Tantra. An image of Ardh-narishvara, an Indian deity representing the androgynous quality of the human psyche. The left side of the body, and thus the right side of the brain, represents the female qualities and the goddess *Shakti; the right side of the body is male and corresponds to *Shiva.*

Abhidhammattha-sangaha

♦

This major work is by Anuruddha (c. 950), an important Buddhist scholar from Sri Lanka. The title translates as "Collection of the Meanings of the Abhidhamma" (see **Tripitaka**), and the text provides an overview of the complete teachings of the Theravada school of *Hinayana Buddhism, with special attention given to what is often called "Buddhist psychology."

Naro Chos-drug

♦

Better known as the Six Doctrines of Naropa, this is the Tibetan name for the major teachings and texts by the *Mahasiddha Naropa (1016–1100), who was also known as the "dauntless disciple." His Six Doctrines (or Yogas) belong to the spiritual heritage of *Vajrayana, and especially to the Shang-pa, *Kagyud-pa, and Rimed schools. At one point Naropa served as the head of the famous Buddhist university at Nalanda, but later he chose to become a student again, this time under Tilopa (988–1069), another of the eighty-four Mahasiddhas.

Some of the teachings in this work are those of the seventh-century, *Bön-influenced **Bardo Thödol;** some are gleaned from the tenth-century **Kalachakra Tantra;** and others belong to the *Inner Tantras and are thus connected to *Dzogchen. The work contains theoretical and practical teachings concerning, for example, one's dream state, the transference of consciousness, and the production of "inner heat."

A translation of a Tibetan commentary on Naropa's doctrines, by the *Gelug-pa reformer Tsongkapa (1357–1419), appears in Charles Muses's *Esoteric Teachings of the Tibetan Tantra.*

Literature

Chang, Garma C.C., trans. *The Six Yogas of Naropa and the Teachings of Mahamudra.* Ithaca, N.Y.: Snow Lion, 1986.

Guenther, Herbert, trans. *The Life and Teaching of Naropa.* Boston and London: Shambhala, 1986.

Muses, Charles A. *Esoteric Teachings of the Tibetan Tantra*. York Beach, Maine: Weiser, 1982.

Lalita Sahasranama

♦

The available translation of this work is based on a manuscript dating from 1785, one the many works of the Indian initiate and scholar Bhaskararaya. The manuscript is, in fact, a late edition with commentaries of a text that is part of the much earlier Brahmanda **Purana** from approximately the eleventh century.

The text is dedicated to the goddess Lalita and consists mainly of listing and explaining the goddess's one thousand names and epithets, a textual procedure common to works of *Tantra and *Shakta. Such "names," consisting of one or more *Sanskrit words, can be very revealing as to the nature and quality of the goddess. They range from "All-pervading," "Multiform," and "Supreme Goddess" to such poetic and descriptive phrases as "the moonlight which gladdens the flowers" or "her breasts are the fruit growing on the creeper-like hair which springs from her deep navel."

Literature
Sastry, R. A., trans. *Lalita Sahasranama*. Nilgiri Hills, India: private printing, 1925. 2nd ed., rev. Delhi: Gian, 1986.

Ching-te ch'uan-teng-lu

♦

This "Record Concerning the Passing On of the Lamp" is the earliest historical work of *Ch'an Buddhism, written in 1004 by the monk Tao-hsüan (not to be confused with the seventh-century Tao-hsuan), who is known as Dosen in Japan. The thirty-volume work, in Japanese known as Denko-roku, contains biographies, anecdotes, and sayings of more than six hundred early masters. Many of the *koans* of Ch'an and *Zen Buddhism, the paradoxical questions that became famous much later, were recorded in these volumes for the first time.

Later collections of this type are the Empo Dento-roku, containing more than one thousand biographies, written by the Japanese monk Shiban Mangen (c. 1625–1710), and the Pi Yän Lu and Wu-men-kuan.

Literature

Chang, Chung-Yuan, trans. *Original Teachings of Ch'an Buddhism: Selected from the Transmission of the Lamp*. New York: Pantheon Books, 1969.

Nila Tantra

◆

A work of twenty-two chapters set in the form of questions posed to *Shiva by the goddess *Parvati, this *Shakta-oriented text was written in the early eleventh century. Apart from a detailed exposition on the value of gurus (male and female teachers), the Nila Tantra speaks of rules concerning purification and the intoning of sacred chants (mantras). Like the Kumari Tantra, this text makes provisions for human victims when discussing sacrifice.

Mila Gnubum and Mila Khabum

◆

The Hundred Thousand Songs of Milarepa (Mila Gnubum) and the Biography of Milarepa (Mila Khabum) are prime examples of a specific type of sacred literature that originates with the eighty-four *Mahasiddhas and similar figures important in the development of *Tantra and *Vajrayana.

The Mila Gnubum represents the complete poetic writings of the famous Tibetan yogi and philosopher Milarepa (c. 1039–1123). The Mila Khabum was written down several decades after Milarepa's death by the so-called Mad Yogi from gTsan. It tells of Milarepa's adventures, hardships, and joys during his personal odyssey toward enlightenment and affords us insight into the style of life, teaching, and initiation during this formative time of Tibetan *Buddhism.

See also **Vajra Songs.**

Literature

Chang, Garma C. C., trans. *The Hundred Thousand Songs of Milarepa.* 2 vols. Boulder: Shambhala, 1971.

Llalungpa, Lobsang P., trans. *The Life of Milarepa.* New York: Dutton, 1977.

Jewel Ornament of Liberation
◆

A twelfth-century text by the Tibetan lama and author Gampopa (1079–1153), a student of the *Mahasiddha Milarepa (see **Mila Gnubum**) and later one of the essential and influential teachers of the *Kagyud-pa lineage. In this text, Gampopa unifies several theories, concepts, and teachings that were becoming separated by the various schools of *Vajrayana that were arising during this early period of Tibetan *Buddhism and *Tantra. He combines Milarepa's *mahamudra,* or *Dzogchen, teachings with the various traditions of his own school. Having been first educated, in his youth, by the Kadam-pa, the school that later gave rise to the *Gelug-pa, he also assimilated this more monastic strand of teachings into his work.

Literature

Guenther, Herbert V., trans. *The Jewel Ornament of Liberation by sGam.Po.Pa.* London: Rider, 1959. Boston and London: Shambhala, 1971.

Li-chiao shih wu-lun
◆

The Treatise on the Foundation of the Way for the Realization of Truth is the basic text of the Ch'üan-chen Tao school of *Taoism. The school, founded in the twelfth century by Wang Ch'un-yang (1112–1170), represents a combination of teachings from Taoism, Confucianism, and *Ch'an Buddhism. The text by Wang Ch'un-yang reflects this mixture and especially discusses the teachings of the **Prajnaparamita Sutra.**

Tannisho

◆

The Tannisho is a collection of sayings, teachings, and precepts by Shonin Shinran (1173–1262), collected and put into writing by his students. Considering that Shinran, in the footsteps of Honen (1133–1212), is a founding teacher of all the Pure Land schools of Japanese *Mahayana Buddhism, this work is regarded by many as an essential sourcebook.

Shinran teaches that even one single recital of a sacred formula, the Nimbutsu, and one single invocation of the associated powers is sufficient in order to attain one's goal. Shinran's teachings state that liberation through personal effort is impossible and that one must turn to divine grace instead. Honen, of whom Shinran was a student, described the recitation method of the Pure Land school as an "easy path" for human living during the "last times" of the world; the expression "last times" refers to the *Kali Yuga.

Literature
Bloom, Alfred. *Shinran's Gospel of Pure Grace.* Tucson: University of
　Arizona Press, 1965.
———. *Tannisho: A Resource for Modern Living.* Honolulu: Buddhist
　Study Center, 1981.

Niruttara Tantra

◆

This relatively short work of fifteen chapters belongs to the *Kula tradition. It is very much a women's *Tantra and is unique in the liberal outlook it takes concerning a woman's lifestyle, a life far less regulated than Indian society would normally permit. The text asserts for women the same sexual freedom as is usually given to male devotees, and in fact states explicitly that "a woman has no fault in being united with a person other than her husband" (S. C. Banerjee, 1988, p. 258). The woman who follows the path of the Kula is sketched in the text as one who roams about freely—in the sense of the independent, not the physical, virgin—and enjoys herself like the goddess *Kali does.

The Niruttara Tantra speaks in detail about important rituals and describes extensively the different "types" of women who often figure in rituals of *Tantra and *Shakta. The text also explains various modes of worship directed to several goddesses, but it especially focuses on Kali, the great "Black Mother of Time, Life, Sexuality, and Death."

The dating of this work is uncertain, but many Kula works originated during the ninth through the twelfth centuries.

Pi Yän Lu

♦

Sometimes spelled Bi Yän Lu, this Chinese "Record of the Blue-Green Cliff" or "Blue Rock Collection" is the probably most famous of books of *Ch'an and *Zen Buddhism. The eleventh-century work represents a compilation of the most poignant and famous *koans of its time. The one hundred koans were compiled by the Chinese master Hsueh-tou Ch'ung-hsien (980–1052), who added a personal commentary to each of the koans. The work soon acquired additional comments and interpretations by another Ch'an master named Yuan Wu (1063–1135). The Japanese title of the work is Hekiganroku.

Literature

Cleary, Thomas, and J. C. Cleary, trans. *The Blue Cliff Record.* Boulder: Shambhala, 1977.

Sekida, Katsuki, trans. *Two Zen Classics: Mumonkan and Hekiganroku.* New York: Weatherhill, 1977.

Sepher ha Zohar. A page from an original Hebrew
edition of the *Sepher ha Zohar.*

Sepher ha Zohar

♦

This Hebrew title, often simply shortened to Zohar, translates as "Book of
Splendor." Written or compiled between 1270 and 1300 by Moses ben
Shem Tov de Leon (c. 1240–1305), the book is regarded by many as the
leading mystical text of the Hebrew cabalah, although **Genesis** and Solomon's

Song of Songs are sometimes regarded as equally important cabalistic texts.

According to its author, the book represents the teachings put forth by a circle of Palestinian adepts in the second and/or third century; the text has thus been written in an artificial form of *Aramaic. Despite justified doubts, the cabalistic tradition has come to accept the Sepher ha Zohar as a genuine text. The concepts and ideas of the work are strongly linked to the Mosaic Torah (see **Old Testament**), but the book also includes other texts—for example, a cabalistic commentary on Solomon's Song.

One of its eighteen chapters, the "Book of Concealment," has some unique information concerning the mystical "Dew of ecstasy" that is produced in the pineal and/or pituitary gland within the human skull. The magical, alchemical atmosphere of this chapter has similarities to the teachings of *Taoism and *Tantra, captured in the following quote: "The Holy One, may He be blessed, does not choose to dwell where the male and female are not united" (Sepher ha Zohar I, 55b).

Literature

Sperling, H., and M. Simon, eds. *The Zohar*. vol. 2. London and New York: Socino Press, 1934.

Kanjur

♦

The Tibetan canon of Buddhist scriptures, compiled and edited under the supervision of the scholar Bu-ston (1290–1364), is known as the Kanjur. The title (Tib., *bKa'-'gyur*) translates as "word of the master" and distinguishes these "received" scriptures from the Tenjur (Tib., *bsTan-'gyur*), the collection of related exegetical works, commentaries, and glossaries that accompany the texts of the Kanjur. Bu-ston, basically a fundamentalist, chose not to include most scriptures of the *Nyingma-pa and all of *Dzogchen in the collection. There is no translation of this huge collection, but the complete Kanjur and Tenjur, 5,104 texts in Tibetan, has been available in recent years in a modern edition of 120 volumes published by Dharma Publications of Berkeley, California.

Kanjur. Sample pages from a Tibetan edition of the Kanjur and Tanjur.

Bön, under pressure from Buddhist competition, classified its own scriptures in two collections with the very same names; the Bön Kanjur, however, contains not Buddha's but *Shenrab's revelations.

Kaulavali Nirnaya Tantra

♦

This text of twenty-two chapters is attributed to the author/adept Jnanananda Paramahansa. This *Tantra is very sexually oriented; it is also notable in its respect for women and its attention to rules and mores concerning social ethics.

The text contains a strange condemnation of sexual union during the daytime and speaks in detail of various Tantrik symbols and rituals. Chapter 4 indicates that, of the five *makara*, sexual union alone will lead the devotee to her or his desired goal. This Tantra of the *Kula school allows, with a few exceptions, promiscuous sexual intercourse with married partners other than one's own, saying that "to the pure in heart everything is pure" (S. C. Banerjee, 1988, p. 217). Chapter 9 states that sexual union is a sin only for the foolish, but that its joys will lead the wise to liberation.

The next chapter condemns some all-too-often encountered features of social life ranging from rape and violence to slander and waste of time. The text further informs us about the status and treatment of women among the Kula: "Respect and consideration for women mark the precepts. All women are to be looked upon as manifestations of the Great Mother. An offending woman should not be beaten even with flowers. A woman of any age, even a girl, or even an uncouth woman should be bidden adieu after salutation" (Banerjee, p. 217).

The remaining chapters are mainly concerned with how to achieve and recognize the various magical or paranormal abilities known as *siddhi.

The Ten Pictures of the Ox

♦

The twelfth-century *Ch'an master Kuo-an Shih-yuan created the original, now long-lost drawings and commentaries known as the Ten Pictures of the Ox, which are sometimes simply referred to as the "Oxherding Pictures." He himself had based this illustrated guide to the realization of truth on earlier versions in which the stages from ignorance to understanding were less clearly defined and in which the allegory consisted of five, or sometimes eight, pictures only. This final version by Kakuan Shien (the author's Japanese name) nonetheless brought the oxherding story to fame and turned it into a widely accepted tool for instruction, inspiring countless masters and students.

The Japanese title for the cycle of pictures and commentaries is Jugyo-no-zu. The Kyoto-based woodblock artist Tomekichiro Tokuriki has executed a series of such oxherding pictures, which appear on the following pages (160–161) and which accompany the texts of Kakuan Shien in Paul Reps's anthology *Zen Flesh, Zen Bones,* in the chapter "Ten Bulls."

尋牛

1. The Search for the Bull

見跡

2. Discovering Footprints

見牛

3. Perceiving the Bull

得牛

4. Catching the Bull

牧牛

5. Taming the Bull

騎牛歸家

6. Riding the Bull Home

7. The Bull Transcended

8. Both Bull & Self Transcended

9. Reaching the Source

10. In the World

The Ten Pictures of the Ox. A series of allegorical woodcarvings that illustrates stages during the search for one's true inner self.

Literature

Reps, Paul, ed. *Zen Flesh, Zen Bones: A Collection of Zen and Pre-Zen Writing.* Rutland, Vt., and Tokyo: C. E. Tuttle Co., 1957. Reprint 1975.

Shobo-genzo

♦

This major work by the widely respected Japanese master Dogen Zenji (1200–1253) is often regarded as the most profound religious work of Japanese Buddhism. Both text and author, though formally belonging to the Soto tradition of *Zen Buddhism, are venerated by most Buddhist schools of Japan.

The work, "A Treasury of the Opened Eye," consists of ninety-five sections and was completed, after a period of twenty-five years, shortly before Dogen's death. It speaks of all aspects of Zen teachings but especially stresses the need for the elimination of all selfish desire, for utter self-surrender and the purification of one's ego.

Dogen Zenji also wrote several more introductory texts, among which one finds a title with a similar name: the Shobo-genzo Zuimonki. Its author, although opposed to all sectarian classifications, nevertheless is now regarded as the founder of the Soto school.

Literature

Cook, Francis Harold. *How to Raise an Ox: Zen Practice As Taught in Zen Master Dogen's Shobogenzo.* Los Angeles: Center Publications, 1978.

Nishiyama, Kosen, and John Stevens, trans. *Shobogenzo: The Eye and Treasury of the True Law.* 3 vols. Sendai, Japan: Daihokkaikaku, 1975–1983.

Yokoi, Yuho, trans. *The Shobo-genzo.* Tokyo: Sankibu Buddhist Bookstore, 1985.

Wu-men-kuan

♦

Compiled by the *Ch'an master Wu-men Hui-k'ai (1183–1260), known in Japan as Mumon Enkai, this originally Chinese work is better known today by its Japanese name Mumonkan. Surpassed only by the Pi Yän Lu (Jap., Hekiganroku), this twelfth-century work is the best collection of poignant and successful *koans (Chin., *kung-an*). The work consists of forty-eight such "riddles" meant to point the mind toward insight, accompanied by commentaries in verse and prose that were added by the compiler.

Literature

Sekida, Katsuki, trans. *Two Zen Classics: Mumonkan and Hekiganroku.* New York: Weatherhill, 1977.
Shibayame, Zenkai. *Zen Comments on the Mumonkan.* New York: Harper & Row, 1974.

Yoga Upanishads

♦

The Yoga Upanishads is a group of twenty-one specific Upanishads that represent commentaries and teachings based on the Yoga Sutra. Most of the texts, mainly written during the fourteenth and fifteenth centuries, are concerned with the yogic systems known as hatha- and *kundalini*-yoga. For a general overview, and a sometimes detailed discussion, of these texts, turn to Georg Feuerstein's *Encyclopedic Dictionary of Yoga* (see Bibliography).

Literature

Ayyangar, T. R. S., trans. *The Yoga Upanishads.* Madras: Adyar Library, 1938. Reprint 1952.

Yogini Tantra

◆

This text contains twenty-eight chapters, the authorship and exact age of which are unknown. To a great extent the text deals with the worship of the goddesses *Kali and *Kamakhya; it describes many of the sacred sites and temples where the goddesses are worshiped, especially those where worship is supposed to have especially excellent results. The text has a number of recommendations concerning the five *makara and about who may perform sexual rituals with whom; it also gives examples of Tantrik visualization techniques.

Like many other *Kula-inspired texts, the Yogini Tantra allows the moral codes of mainstream *Hinduism to be broken and suspends many of the usual rules concerning intermarriage between castes. It allows women to speak up to whomever they choose and to have sexual relations with whomever they please.

There is as yet no complete English translation of the text.

Yoni Tantra

◆

The Yoni Tantra is a religious text from Bengal mainly concerned with describing the yoni *puja*, or "mass of the vulva," one of the more secret and esoteric Tantrik rituals. According to this text, sexual union is an indispensable part of Tantrik ritual and may be performed by and with all women between the ages of twelve and sixty, married or not, except for a woman who is a virgin. The text also explicitly forbids the incestuous mother-son constellation.

In general, however, this *Tantra does not impose many restrictions on the practitioner who is dedicated to the yoni *puja* ritual; it advocates use of the five *makara and leaves the choice of partner, place, and time very much up to the practitioner. The male practitioners are explicitly admonished to treat all women well and never be offensive toward them. "The

*Yoni Tantra. A representation of the divine *yoni, the major object of veneration in rituals described in, for example, the Yoni Tantra. Nineteenth-century woodcarving from Southern India.*

sadhaka who utters the words 'yoni yoni' at the time of his prayers, for him the yoni shall be favorable, granting him enjoyment and liberation" (Yonitantra, Patala III, pp. 53f).

Literature
Schoterman, J. A., trans. *Yonitantra*. New Delhi: Manohar, 1980.

Gheranda Samhita
♦

"Gheranda's Collection" is one of the better known and most recent of the works known as **Samhitas.** Originating in the late seventeenth century, the text has become regarded as one of the major scriptures on classical yoga. The *Vaishnava work is presented as a dialogue between Gheranda, an anonymous sage, and his student. The work is modeled after the fourteenth-century Hatha-Yoga Pradipika and explains a great number of exercises and techniques.

Literature
Vasu, S. Chandra, trans. *Gherandasamhita*. Allahabad: Panini Office, 1914. Reprint. New York: AMS Press, 1974.

Shiva Samhita
♦

This *Sanskrit text of five chapters is of interest mainly to students of hatha-yoga, *Tantra, or both. Its theoretical section, the "Collection of *Shiva's Wisdom," presents a philosophy that is strongly influenced by *Advaita Vedanta; its practical section explains in detail the precepts and rules for the study of yoga and gives clear instructions on how the various steps of yogic development can be achieved.

The text deals with anatomy, breath control, and a large number of exercises and techniques; it also describes the so-called yoni-*mudra,* a Tantrik technique that, according to this **Samhita,** "should not be revealed or given to others." Nonetheless, the text has meanwhile been translated and published and is available to all who can read. In connection with the "secret" exercise, the scripture tells of the splendor of the divine *yoni, which is "brilliant as tens of millions of suns and cool as tens of millions of moons" and explains furthermore that "above the yoni is a very small and subtle flame, whose form is intelligence."

Literature
Vasu, S. Chandra, trans. *Siva Samhita*. Allahabad: Panini Office, 1914. Reprint. New York: AMS Press, 1974.

Adi Granth
♦

This First Book, or Master Book (Granth Sahib), is a compilation of sacred scriptures of the Sikh-Panth, a Hindu/Islamic school founded by Guru Nanak and perpetuated by nine consecutive masters, or gurus. A compilation of these texts, also known as Guru Granth, was first carried out in 1603/1604 by the Guru Arjan (the fifth guru), and it includes writings of Guru Nanak (b. 1469) and of all the Sikh gurus until and including the fifth (the ten gurus of the Sikh are seen as successive incarnations of the first one, the lineage ending in 1708). A later edition of the third century includes texts by the ninth guru (seventeenth century).

The texts are written in a simplified form of Hindi and show a great consistency of diction and spirit despite their multiple authorship. The text's individual hymns are known as *bani* (utterances of the gurus) and are each treated with much reverence.

At the very root of the Sikh's creed are the nonsectarian insights and teachings of Kabir (b. 1440), an Indian mystic poet who strongly influenced Guru Nanak. Kabir's songs and teachings, like his family background, are a mixture of Hinduism and Islam. His (legendary) biography and some of his teachings are part of the Adi Granth.

In a traditional Sikh household, as is in each *gurdwara* (temple), a copy of the Master Book is the central focus of the dwelling.

167

Literature

Khushwant, Singh, trans. *Hymns of Guru Nanak*. New Delhi: Orient Longman, 1969. Reprint. Columbia, Mo.: South Asia Books, 1978.

Macauliffe, Max A. *Sikh Religion: The Gurus, Sacred Writings, and Authors*. 6 vols. Delhi: Low Price Publications, 1990.

Talib, G. S., trans. *Selections from the Holy Granth*. Delhi: Vikhas, 1975.

Trilochan, Singh, et al. *Selections from the Sacred Writings of the Sikh*. London: Allen & Unwin, 1960. Reprint 1974.

Mahanirvana Tantra

◆

In the West this is one of the better-known Tantrik scriptures, mainly by virtue of its early translation by Sir John G. Woodroffe (1865–1936), who wrote under the pseudonym of Arthur Avalon. As S. C. Banerjee states in *A Brief History of Tantra Literature,* however, it is "suspected by some to be a fabrication wholly or partly by Hariharanandanatha" and "designed to bolster up his reformist and radical views."

The text describes, among other things, several important Tantrik rituals and warns that only those who are spiritually developed may engage in sexual rituals. For others, the traditional five *makara are substituted by less "dangerous" practices—eating sweets instead of meat, or praying and chanting instead of engaging in sexual worship. The text also categorically condemns the apparently common practice of having "public women" attend Tantrik rites.

Literature

Woodroffe, Sir John G. *The Great Liberation (Mahanirvana Tantra).* Madras: Ganesh & Co., 1927. Reprint 1985.

Walam Olum

◆

This is one of the few written and published oral traditions coming from

Walam Olum. Cover page of a controversial English transcript of the original pictographs by Constantine S. Rafinesque (d. 1840). The Brinton Collection, Dept. of Special Collections, Van Pelt-Dietrich Library Center, University of Pennsylvania.

tribal people of North America. The manuscript of this work, now in the library of the University of Pennsylvania, has a strange history that has given rise to questions concerning its authenticity, but it is generally regarded as representing the sacred and historical tradition of the Delaware Indians. The text, written in a pictographic, hieroglyph-like language, had first been given to a "white man" by a group of Delaware Indians, also known as Lenape, as a gift and in exchange for his services as a doctor.

The Walam Olum derives its name from the fact that the texts were written in red color on pieces of bark; a literal English translation of the title would be "That Which Is Written in Red." The work itself was put into writing during the eighteenth century and was translated at the beginning of the nineteenth century. No definite date has as yet been assigned to the actual tradition it contains; it may, perhaps, go back as far as the **Tsalagi Teachings.**

Literature

Brinton, Daniel Garrison. *The Lenape and Their Legends.* New York: AMS Press, 1969.

The Book of Mormon

♦

Apart from the **Bible,** the revealed Book of Mormon is the major scripture of the Church of Jesus Christ of Latter-day Saints, a religious movement whose members are commonly known as Mormons. The text, according to members of the church, was revealed in the form of inscribed golden tablets to Joseph Smith (1805–1844) in 1827 at Palmyra, New York. The book is believed to complement the Bible and is said to represent a translation—made by Smith—of inscriptions left by the ancient prophet Mormon that had been hidden at Palmyra for at least one thousand years. The Mormon church thus regards itself as a renaissance of a very early American Christianity that allegedly was established by Christ himself appearing in the New World after his ascension.

In the manner of the ancient prophets, Smith founded the new religion (in 1830) based on his revelation. With his first followers he established a headquarters for the church in Kirtland, Ohio, in 1831, until the fast-growing group—persecuted throughout the country as heretics—moved to Utah and founded Salt Lake City (1847), which is still the Mormon capital. Based on a revelation professed by Smith in 1843, early Mormon teachings included the practice of polygamy, but this aspect was dropped in 1890 under pressure from the general American citizenry.

Literature
Smith, Joseph, Jr., trans. *The Book of Mormon, an account written by the hand of Mormon upon plates taken from the plates of Nephi.* Salt Lake City, Utah: The Church of Jesus Christ of Latter-day Saints, 1986. First edition published in 1830.

Kitab-i-Iqan

♦

This Book of Certitude is one of the fundamental sacred texts of the *Baha'i faith. Among the more than one hundred works by the religion's founder, Baha'u'llah (1817–1892), it is equaled in importance only by the Most Holy Book (Kitab-i-Aqdas), the major repository of Baha'i laws. Of the two, the Book of Certitude (also spelled "Kitabi Ikan") is a more general and probably more accessible work that presents the essential teachings of the faith. In it, Baha'u'llah ("glory of God") speaks extensively on the nature of religion in general and on his concept of god in specific.

Although the Baha'i faith in general is more than tolerant toward other revealed religions—for example, quoting other scriptures during services of worship—the Kitab-i-Iqan itself clearly shows the faith to be an offspring of Islamic thought, mainly combining traditions found in the Qur'an with a few that can be found in the Bible. The fact that orthodox adherents of Islam regard Baha'is as "heretics" is not based on the teachings alone, but also on the fact that Baha'u'llah regarded himself as a prophet—a complete contradiction to Islamic belief.

Literature:
Baha'u'llah. *Kitab-i-Iqan.* 2nd ed. Translated by Shoghi Effendi. Wilmette, Ill.: Baha'i Publishing Trust, 1950.

———. *Tablets of Baha'u'llah Revealed After the Kitab-i-Aqdas.* Translated by Habib Taherzadeh. Haifa: Baha'i World Center, 1978.

———. *Writings of Baha'u'llah: A Compilation.* New Delhi: Baha'i Publishing Trust, 1986.

Kalevala

♦

This collection of old songs from northern Europe is especially associated with Finland, where the text came to be regarded as a national epic. The work was compiled and published in the nineteenth century by Elias Lönnrot (1802–1884), but it includes older material. The author actually traveled up and down the country listening to the memorized songs of then still living bards, thus recording the oral tradition of Finnish and northern Russian peoples of earlier times. After a first, short version of about 12,000 lines in 1835, Lönnrot continued his collection and fourteen years later presented a longer version that contains 22,795 lines of poetry and song.

The Kalevala speaks of gods and of heroes whose lives are a continuous battle, both physical and magical, against the forces of darkness. As a whole, it should be regarded as a partly fictional nineteenth-century work of which about one third is clearly the poetic invention of the author.

Glossary

Advaita Vedanta The *Sanskrit term *advaita* means "non-two-ness," and Advaita Vedanta translates as "the nondual end of the Vedas." The term refers to the various schools of *Hinduism that are marked by a strong or exclusively nondualist philosophy, based on the metaphysics expounded in the **Vedas, Upanishads,** and related scriptures.

Often the expression is used as a name for the absolute nondualist teachings of Shankara (c. 788–822), a system also known as Kevala Advaita. According to this philosopher, all of reality is fundamentally united—one, not two—and essentially divine.

See also *Vedanta.

Aramaic Originally the language of a branch of Semitic peoples from the Syrian desert, Aramaic became the lingua franca of the Near East. It was written in a Phoenician script that turned out to be one of the most influential in the history of writing, functioning as a blueprint for most of the alphabets of Roman-influenced Western and Indian-influenced Eastern languages.

Baha'i Faith This is a relatively new religious movement founded by the mystic Baha'u'llah (1817–1892), an inspired disciple of the Bab (d. 1850). Coming from a *Shi'ite background, the Bab regarded himself as a prophet who superseded the Islamic prophet Muhammad and all previous religious founders. The Bab saw himself as someone who prepared the way for a new faith, Baha'i, which should not be confused, as sometimes happens, with the Babi faith or Babism.

The Baha'i creed incorporated some teachings of the other major religions yet presents itself an "independent world religion," sometimes symbolized by nine-sided sacred buildings. The faith has adherents in virtually every country and has major temples, called Houses of Worship, in the United States, Israel, Uganda, India, Germany, and Panama, to name but a few.

Bodhisattva(s) The "bodhisattva ideal" of the *Mahayana schools of *Buddhism, based on the stories of the various bodhisattvas, is one of compassionate love for all fellow beings. It requires that someone who attains enlightenment refrains from collecting the potential fruit of her or his efforts—that is, individual liberation from the wheel of rebirth—and instead returns to life in order to help others attain the same goal.

Most often the term is used for a number of male deities such as Manjushri, Avalokiteshvara, or Maitreya. The only better-known female bodhisattva is the Chinese/Japanese Kwan Yin, or Kannon, the Indo-Tibetan Avalokiteshvara as bodhisattva of compassion. She too, however, is often presented as, or said to be, androgynous. The **Bardo Thödol** does mention eight female bodhisattvas who appear in groups of two during the second and fifth day of the *bardo*.

Bön (Tib., "invocation") This is the name for the pre-Buddhist, shamanic religious traditions of the Tibetan Himalayas. Many teachings and rituals of Bön were finally absorbed into Tantrik *Buddhism. The unorganized shamans and magicians lost ground, and believers, when Indian Tantrik masters began teaching in Tibet during the seventh and eighth centuries. By 779, *Vajrayana had risen to the position of state religion; meanwhile, a movement known as Reformed Bön evolved, which by late in the eighth century was grudgingly accepted and allowed to operate in Tibet. In the centuries that followed Bön developed alongside early *Vajrayana, and sometimes their teachings were similar, each influencing the other. By the eleventh century Reformed Bön had gained some ground, and its teachings have been transmitted ever since.

Brahmanism This term is used to indicate the specific religious beliefs

174

and practices prevalent in India before and during the formative years of *Buddhism (c. 500 B.C.E.–100 C.E.). An orthodox form of *Hinduism, it derives its name from the highest members of India's caste system, the priests known as Brahmins, and from the Indian concept of *brahman* (see **Brahmanas**). Brahmanism was mainly concerned with the various rituals and sacrifices proscribed by the **Vedas** and took strong opposition to later developments such as *Shakta and *Tantra.

Buddhism The *buddha-dharma* (Buddha teaching), like most other religions, is not as homogenous as it may seem to an outsider on first sight. The teachings of Siddhartha Gautama (563–483 B.C.E.), the historical Buddha, have been adapted to many societies and been influenced by many local customs and beliefs. Though Buddhism originally developed in India, the major Buddhist countries today are Bhutan, Burma, Japan, Kampuchea, Korea, Laos, Malaysia, Mongolia, Nepal, Sri Lanka, Taiwan, Thailand, Tibet, and Vietnam. In India itself it has played only a marginal role since the thirteenth century, and it exists today mainly in those Himalayan territories that were politically incorporated into the giant country in relatively recent times: Northern Assam, Darjeeling, Ladakh, and Sikkim.

Basically, Buddhism has two major subdivisions, known as *Hinayana and *Mahayana, a division that arose in the first century C.E. Two other terms nonetheless often appear in articles and books—*Vajrayana and *Ch'an (*Zen). Formally, these two schools are part of Mahayana, yet by virtue of their large sphere of influence they are often regarded as equally major divisions of Buddhism as a whole.

Buddhism—especially Mahayana divisions such as Zen and Vajrayana—today attracts growing numbers of adherents in Europe and the United States. The number of people within the fold of Buddhism is about 250 to 500 million.

Ch'an This shortened form of the Chinese term *ch'an-na* ("meditative attention") is based on the *Sanskrit *dhyana* ("meditation"). It has become the general name for a religious and philosophical movement in China that developed when *Mahayana Buddhism, imported from India beginning in the first century C.E., met with Chinese *Taoism. When the Ch'an tradition reached Japan, during and after the twelfth century, it became known there as *Zen. Today, the two terms are often used as synonyms, but a distinction should be made between Ch'an or Zen depending on the cultural context in question. Ch'an also has been—and still is—active in Korea and Taiwan. All schools of Ch'an and Zen trace their lineage back to the Indian traveler and Buddhist master Bodhidharma (c. 470–543), the twenty-eighth patriarch of Indian Buddhism and the first patriarch of Ch'an, and ultimately to the historical Buddha. For the development of the various schools within the fold of Ch'an/Zen, see chart 4 on page 197. For a very detailed lineage chart, including all important masters, see the *Encyclopedia of Eastern Philosophy and Religion* by Ingrid Fischer-Schreiber, et al. (see Bibliography).

Coptic   This term is used to indicate that the Egyptian language has been written down using the letters of the Greek alphabet. It is not a specific language or system of writing unto itself.

Dzogchen   This is the Tibetan term for the class of the "higher" or *Inner Tantras, known in *Sanskrit as *ati-yoga*. Dzogchen teachings have been transmitted mainly within the *Nyingma-pa and *Kagyud-pa schools of *Vajrayana. The essentially nonsectarian tradition is still alive today. Dzogchen (Tib., Dzogs-chen, sometimes also transliterated as Dzokchen, Dzog Chen, or Zogqen) was sometimes regarded as a heretic school, and its texts and teachings were consciously left out of the Buddhist **Kanjur,** a collection of sacred texts edited by the fundamentalist Bu-ston. Nonetheless, adherents of the *Gelug-pa and other schools have recognized the value and power of Dzogchen and have often practiced its teachings, as did the fifth Dalai Lama, for example; if necessary they did so in secret.

Dzogchen attempts to present a middle path between the gradual (*Hinayana and *Mahayana) and sudden (*Ch'an) schools, teaching that "the starting point is the goal." A detailed discussion of the school's precepts and techniques can be found in *Sky Dancer* by Keith Dowman (see Bibliography).

176

Fang-chung shu   This general term from early *Taoism is used to indicate all the sexual exercises and techniques that lead to mystical union with the *Tao and/or to achieving immortality.

The philosophy underlying such exercises is based on the concept that the union of Heaven (male) and Earth (female) gave rise to all things and to all beings. Adepts of *fang-chung shu,* both female and male, partake of that primordeal creative process by once more, on a human scale, repeating and reenacting this union, thereby experiencing the Tao and uniting with its flow of energy. The various techniques and rituals of *fang-chung shu* were practiced both privately and publicly until about the seventh century, when a dominant Confucian morality outlawed such practices.

Gelug-pa   This school, the "Model of virtue," is the best-known school of *Vajrayana today. The Gelug-pa, sometimes simply referred to as the Yellow Hat school, is rooted in the earlier Kadham-pa tradition and in that school's reformation under Tsongkapa (1357–1419), a teacher who preferred strict, monastic discipline and who found the Kadham-pa monks not yet virtuous enough.

After the foundation of the first Gelug-pa monastery in 1409, the school expanded during the fifteenth century, with the building of many more strongholds throughout Tibet. Around 1475, a violent struggle for power broke out between the Gelug-pa and other schools, and a true consolidation of Gelug-pa power came only during 1642–1659 under the fifth Dalai Lama. This included confiscation of non-Gelug monasteries and even the burning of books.

The Gelug-pa emphasized the study of logic and philosophy and became the dominating force in Tibet, assuming both religious and secular leadership. The Gelug-pa teachings are continued mainly through the lineage of the Dalai Lama and are still alive in Tibet, Nepal, Northern India, and in some Western countries.

Gnosticism   This is the collective term for a great variety of schools that arose during the early days of Christianity, mainly in Syria and Egypt. Gnosticism has spiritual and philosophical roots not only in Christianity,

177

but also in the teachings and religious beliefs of Greece, Egypt, the Near East, Persia, and India. Most of the believers in *gnosis* ("higher spiritual knowledge") were seen as heretics by the fathers of the Christian church: it was not only the Gnostics' insistence on knowledge rather than blind faith as the main spiritual goal and achievement but also certain rituals practiced by some of their sects that caused them to be declared heretic.

Probably the most important Gnostic text is the **Pistis Sophia,** but most contemporary information on Gnostic teachings comes from collections of texts such as the **Nag Hammadi Sciptures** or the **Corpus Hermeticum.**

See also *Mandaeans.

Hinayana This "small, or lesser, vehicle" indicates the southern branch of *Buddhism that developed in India and Sri Lanka and then spread to several Southeast Asian countries. Originally the term was used, almost depreciatingly, by adherents of the then-arising *Mahayana school, and Hinayanists themselves prefer to refer to their teachings as *Theravada.

The development of Hinayana took place during the centuries following the death of Siddhartha Gautama Shakyamuni Buddha (in 483 B.C.E.). Out of the original Buddhist community arose several separate schools brought about by disagreements in interpreting the Buddha's teachings, a development that ultimately also led to the rise of *Mahayana. Of all the once existing Hinayana schools (see chart 1 on page 194), only *Theravada has truly survived and is still active today in countries such as Burma, Kampuchea, Laos, Sri Lanka, and Thailand.

Hinduism This is an almost outdated and very general term that often indicates little more than that a certain school has come forth out of India, a country that virtually teems with different religious systems, sects, and schools. Using the term Hindu to describe a person would indicate essentially that she or he is not a member of the *Jaina or *Sikh religions, nor of *Buddhism, Islam, or Christianity—the other major religions existing in India. The major traditions of Hindu worship practiced today are *Shaiva, *Vaishnava, *Shakta, and *Tantra. Historically speaking, Hinduism has been strongly shaped by what is now known as *Brahmanism and *Vedanta, the ancient teachings that developed in India with the invading Aryans (during and after the fifteenth century B.C.E.).

Inner Tantras This is the name for the highest of the four classes of Buddhist *Tantra, which emphasizes nonaction and the identity of path and goal. To this class belong the classical texts of the *Mahasiddhas such as the **Guhyasamaja Tantra, Hevajra Tantra,** and Samvara Tantra. The teachings of the Inner Tantras, also known as *Dzogchen or *mahamudra,* represent the highest possible achievement, when path and goal merge at the apex of the worshiper's spiritual development, and are said to lead to true Buddhahood.

Jaina or Jainism This orthodox, yet non-Vedic religion was founded by the Indian ascetic Vardhamana (540–468 B.C.E.), better known as Mahavira (Skt., "great hero") and a contemporary of the historical Buddha. Two major facets of the Jaina teachings are strict adherence to the practice of noninjury of any living being and the belief that the truly divine dwells within an individual's soul rather than in "outside" agents such as a god or goddess. Mahatma Gandhi (1869–1948), the famous strategist of nonviolence, was strongly influenced by the Jainas. In 1984 India had more than three million Jaina practitioners.

Kagyud-pa This is one of the major schools of *Vajrayana Buddhism, the name of which means "oral transmission" in Tibetan. Among the members of this school were many inventive and nonconformist monks and masters, and their activities led to a variety of separate schools: the so-called four major and eight lesser ones. Of these schools, only a few survive today in countries and regions such as Sikkim, Bhutan, Nepal, and Ladakh; practitioners of this school can also be found in Europe and the United States.

One of the major figures in the Kagyud tradition is Gampopa (1079–1153), who founded the school in 1125 and whose roots are traced to several of the *Mahasiddhas. More than other Tibetan schools, the Kagyud-pa have incorporated and transmitted many of the teachings from original *Bön and *Tantra, as well as a number of traditions of the early *Nyingma-pa. The school's teachings include, among others, many *Dzogchen traditions and the **Naro Chos-drug.**

In a fashion similar to the **Mila Gnubum**—the songs of Milarepa (1039–1123)—most of the important Kagyud masters have composed teaching songs, oral transmissions that are discussed under **Vajra Songs.**

Kali Kali is the Indian deity who is often regarded as a dark, black (Skt., *kala*), and destructive goddess of time and death (see illustration on page 139). To her worshipers in both *Hinduism and *Tantra, however, she represents a multifaceted Great Goddess responsible for all aspects of life from conception to death. Although Kali is worshiped throughout India and Nepal, she is most popular in Bengal, where one also finds her most famous temple, Kalighat, near Calcutta.

Kali Yuga This is the era considered by Hindu tradition to be the most degenerated of all cosmic ages. The Kali Yuga began in 3102 B.C.E., around the time that humanity began writing, and has an expected duration of 432,000 years. At the end of this age, according to the tradition, the world's dissolution will come by fire.

Kamakhya Kamakhya represents the physical aspect of the Great Goddess Mahamaya when she is prepared for sexual enjoyment. In such depiction, she is often shown standing on a red lotus with a garland in her hand. Her steeds are both the Lion(ess) and the Bull. The goddess is thought to dwell at the Kamakhya Pitha in Assam, where she is revered as the menstruating *yoni of the earth.

Koan This is the Japanese transliteration for the Chinese *kung-an,* a term used to indicate a paradoxical saying, a sophisticated "riddle" designed to baffle or boggle the mind. *Koans* are highly valued in *Ch'an and *Zen Buddhism, where they are used to point a student toward an essential insight—beyond the confines of logic and linear reasoning—and, through practice, ultimately toward enlightenment. *Koans* have been collected in works such as the **Pi Yän Lu** and the **Wu-men-kuan.** Among the schools of Japanese *Zen, the Rinzai (founded in 1191) especially values the use of *koans.*

Kula **or** *Kaula* This is the most influential of the so-called left-hand, or *Vamacara, sects of Tantrism. The term is also used to designate a member of the Kula family, a particularly widespread group of Tantriks in which membership is gained either by birth or initiation.

Mahasiddhas In contrasting to the scholastic and academically oriented Buddhist tradition between the sixth and twelfth centuries in India, the Mahasiddhas essentially represent the path of self-realization through personal experience. These "greatly (*maha*) accomplished ones (*siddha,* see *siddhi*)" were not monks, but rather they were adepts of spontaneity and individuality. The experiences, attainments, and teachings of these eighty men and four women, who came from a wide spectrum of social backgrounds and who followed the path of the Tantrik yogi/magician in order to attain liberation and enlightenment within one lifetime, are the root of *Vajrayana.

The exact genealogy and historical dates of the Mahasiddhas are not totally clear. Most lived between 750 and 1150 and the best "scientific guess" about their genealogy is offered by Keith Dowman in his *Masters of Mahamudra* (1985). The tradition of the Mahasiddhas has been carried through time mainly by the *Nyingma-pa and the *Kagyud-pa schools of Tibetan Buddhism.

See **Vajra Songs.**

Mahayana This is the so-called greater vehicle and the major, northern branch of *Buddhism that originally was prevalent in India along with *Hinduism and the *Jaina religion. Beginning in the first century, its teachings spread in several waves to Burma, China, Indonesia, Japan, Korea, Mongolia, Nepal, Taiwan, Thailand, Tibet, and Vietnam, countries in which Mahayana came to flourish and where it gave rise to a great variety of schools.

181

The term is used to differentiate these teachings from those of the earlier *Hinayana, from which it developed during the first century. The concept of Mahayana Buddhism as a "great vehicle" refers to its many-sided approach to liberation, offering different ways and means for different types of people; "types" in this instance refers to psychological makeup rather than to gender, caste, nationality, or race.

The Mahayana teachings have developed into many offshoots (see chart 2 on page 195) and comprise such different schools as *Vajrayana of Northern India, Tibet, and neighboring regions; the schools of *Ch'an and Pure Land Buddhism in China; the *Zen lineages; *Tantra-influenced schools in Japan; and the Buddhist folk religions of Korea and Taiwan.

Makara This is the technical term for the five "basic ingredients" of many rituals of the *Vamacara Tantrik tradition. The Kamakhya Tantra clearly defines the five *makaras,* as quoted in Benjamin Walker's *Tantrism:* "The true devotee should worship the Mother of the Universe with liquor, fish, meat, cereal, and copulation" (1982, p. 65). The *makaras* are also known as the "five *M*s" because their *Sanskrit names, here in the order of the list above, begin with that letter: *madya, matsya, mamsa, mudra,* and *maithuna.*

Mandaeans From the *Aramaic for "gnosis," this is the name for the only actively surviving school of *Gnosticism, which in 1982 had about 15,000 members in Iraq and Iran. Their teachings are contained in the **Ginza** and in the lesser-known Book of Johannes. The Mandaean redeemer is known as Manda, or Hibil-Ziwa, who is thought to have incarnated several times—for example as Abel, Enoch, and John the Baptist. His opponent, the chief of evil, is the demiurge Ptah-il, who not only created the world but who does not cease to misguide humanity by incarnating as false prophets—for example in the figures of Abraham, Moses, Jesus, and Muhammad.

Mi-tsung The Chinese School of Secrets, which represents a *Tantra-oriented *Buddhism, originated in the eighth century, when Indian Tantriks came to China. Here the school soon lost its influence, yet it lived on in Japan as *Shingon. From the seventh through the tenth centuries, Mi-tsung was also very active in Korea.

Nyingma-pa This oldest school of Tibetan *Buddhism—the "ancient ones" or "old order"—bases its teachings on the early influx (eighth and ninth centuries) of the then-new *Vajrayana teachings, a process known as the first diffusion. The Nyingma-pa represents the earliest and nonmonastic school of Tantrik Buddhism, the adherents of which were mainly wandering yogis, magicians, and exorcists, often with close ties to the shamanic *Bön-po. Only in the early fourteenth century did the Nyingmas organize into a monastic order, forced to do so by a need to compete with the other powerful schools then active in Tibet. Traditional texts of this school are, for example, **The Life and Liberation of Padmasambhava** and **The Secret Life and Songs of Lady Yeshe Tsogyal.**

Orphic Mysteries What are known as the Orphic Mysteries are the ritual celebrations of a mystery religion based on both Greek and Egyptian beliefs, deities, and symbols. Orphism was a religion that developed during the fifth century B.C.E. and attempted to combine the mysteries of Apollo with those of Dionysus. It centerd around the legends of the singer Orpheus, with an androgynous, hermaphrodite god Eros often becoming a main character.

The Orphic Mysteries were directed toward personal initiation and the attainment of a blameless life, without which the believer would eternally return to the world. During his or her initiation into the Orphic Mysteries, the candidate had to enter the earth (symbolic death), come out once more (rebirth), and would then partake of the milk from the Earth Mother's breasts. Texts used in such mysteries are known as **Orphic Hymns.**

Pahlavi This Persian language, also known as Pehlevi or Middle Persian, is part of the Indo-European language family. Pahlavi is also the name of a Persian ruling dynasty that began in the late nineteenth century and ended in 1980.

Pali   Related to *Sanskrit, Pali was the vernacular language of Northern India during the time when *Buddhism arose in India. It is therefore the language of many early Buddhist scriptures, especially those of the *Hinayana branch.

Parvati   The goddess Parvati is regarded as a personification or "daughter" of the Himalayas and represents *Shakti in one of her many manifestations as partner and lover of *Shiva. The **Nila Tantra** and a number of other Indian sacred texts are written in the form of questions and answers passing between Shiva and Parvati.

Prakrit   This is the comprehensive term for languages and dialects of the specifically Indic group of the Indo-European languages. The term also signifies a "natural" language as opposed to a consciously designed one such as *Sanskrit; the Sanskrit word *prakriti* means "nature" and/or "creatrix."

Sanskrit   Sanskrit is the sacred language of India in which most of its religious texts are written. The term itself means "perfect" and "complete," apt to describe a "language of the gods," or Devanagari, as it also called. Since the language was designed and developed along with the philosophical, scientific, and religious thought of India, it features a highly differentiated and sophisticated terminology for extraordinary states of consciousness, subtle physiology, and mental/spiritual processes of which no immediate equivalents exist in Western languages.

Sarvastivada   This *Hinayana school reached its height of activity around the sixth and seventh centuries. It was active in the development of *Buddhism in Burma, Indonesia, and Kampuchea and, with others, was instrumental in the rise of *Mahayana.

Shaiva or *Shaivism*   This is the comprehensive name for the teachings of a great number of schools in India, and especially in Kashmir, whose common denominator is the worship and veneration of the god *Shiva as principal reality and sole possessor of power. Shaiva, as a movement, has often rivaled *Shakta and *Vaishnava; there are also groups who attempted to merge the views of these systems. Little of the vast literature of the Shaivas is extant and/or has been researched, translated, and published. In a number of works the Shaiva movement is often referred to as *pancaratra* tradition.

Shakta One of the later-developed religious systems within *Hinduism, Shakta designates the worship of *Shakti as the principal deity and energy of the universe and creation. The creative force is recognized as being sexual in nature and is therefore often represented in images of sexual union, similar to Tantrik practice. Various subschools may use teachings that mirror this on the physical plane by using sexuality in their rituals; others see it as mere symbology and reject all actual union. One clearly delineated difference between *Tantra and Shakta is that Shakta teachings always regard the feminine principle—*Shakti or Devi—as supreme, whereas in Tantra the devotee is more or less free to choose whether *Shiva, Shakti, or neither is so regarded.

Shakti This is the name for a complex concept and the supreme goddess of *Shakta and *Tantra. Both as a goddess and a symbol Shakti represents the ultimate female principle of energy and motion, the primal cause of all and everything without which there could be no manifested universe. Her name is in fact the *Sanskrit feminine noun that might be translated into English as "creative energy" and/or "power."
See also *Kali, *Shiva.

Shenrab Shenrab is the adept regarded as the founder of the indigenous Tibetan *Bön religion. It is as yet undecided (by Western scientists) whether he was a third-century Bön priest/magician or merely a legendary figure invented to equal the Buddhist's historical Buddha. His revelations are contained in the Bön version of the **Kanjur**.

Shi'ites or Shi'ite Islam Sometimes called Schiism, this is the second-largest subdivision of Islam, which differs from the *Sunni majority in its beliefs regarding the legitimate succession of the teachings after the prophet Muhammad's death in 632. The Shi'ites consider the only rightful heir of the prophet to have been the caliph Ali ibn Abu Tarib (600–661), related to Muhammad by a marriage with the prophet's daughter Fatima.

Today, Shi'ite Islam (85,000 members in 1988) is practiced mainly in Iran, Iraq, Lebanon, and Bahrain; in the 1980s and 1990s it gained influence through fundamentalist revival movements in various Islamic countries.

Shingon The teachings of Shingon, a Japanese school (the True Word) of *Mahayana orientation, derive from the Chinese *Mi-tsung and show many influences from *Tantra and *Vajrayana. Founded by Kobo Daishi (774–835), better known as Kukai, the school is divided into *ken-kyo* (exoteric teachings) and *mitsou-kyo* (esoteric teachings). Shingon today is one of the largest Buddhist schools in Japan.

Shinto The Chinese term for the indigenous, nature-oriented Japanese religion, Kami-no-Michi, Shinto translates as the "way of the divine." The main deity of Shinto is the goddess Amaterasu—representing the sun—and its main shrine is at Ise, near Kyoto. Although there are at least 130 different sects, Japan also knew a "state Shinto" until it was suppressed by the American army in the wake of World War II.

Shiva The Indian male creative principle and the opposite pole and partner/lover of *Shakti, Shiva is known under many names and has many functions and attributes, which differ from school to school and sect to sect. He is worshiped all over India and in neighboring countries, but especially among the non-Islamic population of Kashmir. Shiva and *Parvati, another aspect of Shakti, are often featured in sacred texts as a conversing couple, one answering the other's questions and thus instructing their devotees.

Siddhis This is the *Sanskrit term for a type of spiritual/mental accomplishment best approximated with a modern English expression such as ESP (extrasensory perception) and/or with concepts such as "mystical power," "paranormal potential," and "magical skill."

The term *siddhi* is also the root of the title for the "greatly accomplished ones," or ★Mahasiddhas, each or whom had achieved one or more of these "perfections." ★Vajrayana texts speak of eight types of *siddhi* only, but one can find a much more detailed classification in the Hindu ★Tantras, where eighty-four are recognized. Among these, several phenomena can be found which correspond to those charted by contemporary parapsychology—for example, psychokinesis, telekinesis, and the astral "double."

Soma A sacred drug used by early shamans, yogis, and Brahmins, soma was probably derived from *Amanita muscaria,* a mushroom also known as fly agaric. The same drug was known to the ancient Persians as *haoma.*

In Indian subtle physiology, the term is used to refer to the "nectar of ecstasy," a fluid and/or energy stimulated and released through certain psychophysical techniques.

Sunni This is the largest of the two major subdivisions of Islam. The school's name derives from the Arabic *sunna* (rule), a term for the body of traditional laws which evolved from the teachings of Muhammad. Sunnites regard the first three caliphs as the rightful successors of the prophet, the major difference in doctrine that divides them from the ★Shi'ite school. The Sunnis are often described as the orthodox school of Islam, yet developments in the twentieth century have shown that they in fact are more liberal and adaptive than the much more orthodox Shi'ites.

Sutra Fundamental religious, sacred texts (Skt., "thread"), *sutras* are regarded as divine revelation. The term's application has, however, widened considerably, and many *sutras* are, in fact, compact summaries of other, earlier, and more lengthy scriptures.

Tantra A mystical/spiritual system of psychology, philosophy, and cosmology, Tantra aims at the union of opposites on all levels of being and becoming, from cosmic to quantum levels and on astral, mental, and physical planes. This central theme is expressed in many sacred texts, as well as in art, alchemy, science, and ritual observance. Women and men are seen as microcosmic expressions and/or as mirrors of macrocosmic energies represented by the goddess *Shakti and the god *Shiva, in whatever guise they may appear (see also *Vajrayana, *Vamacara).

The term is also used to indicate a sacred treatise containing spiritual and psychophysical teachings concerned with the transmutation of energy, liberation of the mind, attainment of one's full potential, and other Tantrik practices (see also *Inner Tantras).

Tao A word meaning "way" and/or "teaching," this Chinese term now designates the main concept of *Taoism. In the **Tao-te Ching**, this term was used for the first time in such a metaphysical sense, referring to an all-embracing first principle and primordial source of all things. Although there have been many attempts at defining and explaining the Tao, one of its basic characteristics is that it cannot be narrowly defined; it is nameless and unnamable.

Taoism Based on the idea of the *Tao, this influential and original system of Chinese religion, philosophy, and inner alchemy has strongly shaped the whole of Chinese culture.

What we call Taoism—usually rather indiscriminately—consists of two major streams of thought, lifestyle, and practice. One branch, Tao-chia, represents the philosophical and mystical branch and is based on classical Taoist texts such as the **Tao-te Ching** and the Inner Chapters of the **Chuang-tzu**. The other branch, Tao-chiao, can best be described as the more religious, magical, and alchemical branch of Taoism; its teachings include those of the philosophical branch but its roots also go back to more ancient Chinese traditions. One of the oldest texts of this tradition is the **Nei P'ing** of Ko Hung (284–364).

See also *Fang-chung shu.

Terma (Tib., "treasure") These secret treasures in the form of "hidden texts" were intended to be rediscovered at a future time by an inspired *terton*, or "revealer." According to *Vajrayana tradition, such texts were prepared, sealed, and hidden by ancient teachers such as Padmasambhava and Yeshe Tsogyal during the time that *Buddhism, after a relatively short flowering, was threatened and outlawed in Tibet.

See also the section in the introduction "Of Canons, Hidden Texts, and the Burning of Books."

Terton (Tib., "revealer of treasure") This is the term for those people who allegedly "rediscover" previously "hidden" sacred texts (*terma*). According to legend, such texts had been hidden to preserve them for future generations. Members of the *Nyingma-pa and *Bön also used this "hide and recover" method during the various phases of persecution these groups had to survive.

Theravada Originally just one of several *Hinayana schools (see chart 1 on page 194), Theravada today is used almost as a synonym for Hinayana; this is largely because Theravada is the only surviving school of this early Buddhist tradition. The major countries where the Theravada school is still dominant are Sri Lanka (since 250 B.C.E.), Burma (since the eleventh century), and Kampuchea and Thailand (both since the thirteenth century).

Vaipulya Sutras This is the general term used for a group of important, extensive (Skt., *vaipulya*) texts of *Mahayana Buddhism, each of which features a specific aspect of its general teachings. Among these are the **Avatamsaka Sutra**, the **Prajnaparamita Sutra**, and the Ratnakuta Sutra. Other such *vaipulya *sutras* are found in the Chinese canon only. These are the Mahaparinirvana Sutra, the Mahasamnipata Sutra, and the **Lotus Sutra**.

Vaishnava or Vaishnaism Centered around the god Vishnu, Vaishnava is one of the great Indian theistic religious traditions; it is also known by the names Pancaratra or Bhagavata. Together with its main rival, the *Shaiva tradition, Vaishnava was instrumental in the development of the Indian systems of Yoga. Probably the best text of this tradition is the **Bhagavadgita,** but the school has also brought forth more than two hundred works known under the collective name of **Samhitas.**

Vajrayana The Diamond Vehicle, Vajrayana is the name for the esoteric, *Tantra-influenced *Buddhism of Tibet, Bhutan, Nepal, Ladakh, and Mongolia. The term distinguishes it from *Hinayana and *Mahayana, though Vajrayana itself is also a subdivision of the latter. In early studies on Tibetan Buddhism by Europeans and Americans, it has sometimes wrongly been called Lamaism. Applied to Christianity, this would result in a religion named Priestism or Bishopism.

The Diamond Vehicle is most often said to consist of four schools, the *Nyingma-pa, Saskya-pa, *Kagyud-pa, and *Gelug-pa, yet there are also more than twenty other (sub)groups and schools (see chart 3 on page 196). For several centuries the Gelug-pa has been the largest and most dominant school of Tibetan Buddhism in Tibet itself and has been the best known in the West mainly because the Dalai Lama, the traditional spiritual and political leader of Tibet, comes from this background.

Vamacara This is the "left-hand" path of *Tantra, in which worship often includes actual sexual union. Followers of this path are called Vamacharis or Vamacharias. This school must be considered as representing the original Tantra and *Shakta—there is no mention of a "right-hand" Dakshinacara or Dakshinamarga before the thirteenth century, although the centuries during which Tantrism mainly developed and flourished begin with the fourth or fifth. The designation "left" derives from the fact that the women participating in the rites were seated to the left of their male partners.

Vedanta (Skt., "end of the Vedas") This is the comprehensive term for the philosophical and metaphysical concept that originated with the **Vedas** and **Upanishads.** It is the dominant philosophy of *Brahmanism, or early

*Hinduism, and its main concept is a nondualist interpretation of the universe and all phenomena.

See also *Advaita Vedanta.

Yab-yum This Tibetan term, literally translated, means "father-mother" and is a symbol for ritual sexual union and/or the union of opposites. In the typical *yab-yum* pose, the couple is facing each other with the woman sitting on the man's lap. Deities in this position, often found in sculptures and paintings, can be found in almost every temple and monastery of *Vajrayana affiliation.

Yogacara or Yogachara (Skt., "application of Yoga") This school within the fold of early *Mahayana Buddhism is also known by the name Vijnanavada, or "the school that teaches knowledge." The school's main teaching explains that everything, including the phenomena of the world and all experience, is simply a projection of the mind. The *Sanskrit term *yoga*, as used here, does include all kinds of meditative practices and one's striving toward becoming a *bodhisattva. The school was founded by Asanga and others in the fourth century.

See Avatamsaka Sutra.

Yogini In both Hindu and Buddhist *Tantra, this term is used not only to indicate a specific "class" of female deities, but also as a title for female participants in certain Tantrik rituals.

Sometimes the term also refers to particular accomplished female ascetics who spread Tantrik knowledge among the masses; it is used for a shamaness or medicine woman and can sometimes indicate a woman possessed by the goddess.

See also **Yogini Tantra.**

Yoni This is a reverent *Sanskrit term for the vulva, the visible outer genitals of a woman or goddess; the word is sometimes also used to mean the complete female genital system.

Zen This term is an abbreviation of the Japanese *zenna* or *zenno*, meaning "meditation." The name is used to indicate the system of teachings that developed in Japan when Chinese *Ch'an Buddhism, part of the *Mahayana tradition, arrived there during the twelfth and thirteenth centuries. During its formative period, Japanese Zen developed into various schools and subschools, all of which nonetheless trace their lineages back to Daruma—the Japanese name for the patriarch Bodhidharma (c. 470–543)—and thus to the historical Buddha.

See also *koan.*

The Development of the
Buddhists Schools

The following charts on the development of *Buddhism and its schools have been provided in order to enable the reader to place its sacred texts into the developmental context of this religion, which has given rise to an extraordinarily large number of schools and sects.

Chart 1: Hinayana

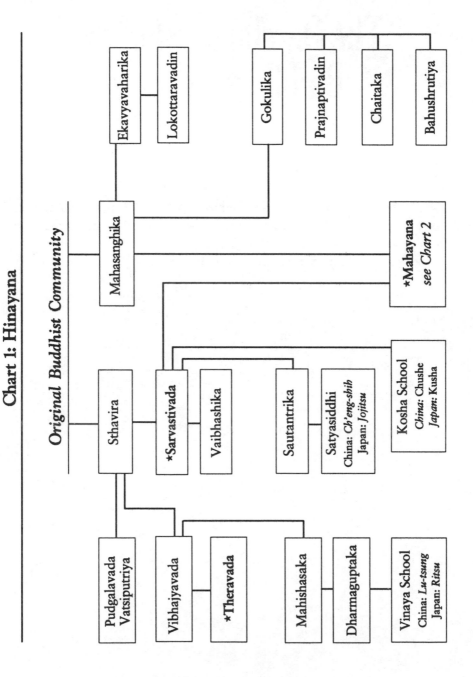

Original Buddhist Community

Mahasanghika
- Ekavyavaharika
  - Lokottaravadin
- Gokulika
  - Prajnaptivadin
  - Chaitaka
  - Bahushrutiya
- *Mahayana see Chart 2

Sthavira
- Pudgalavada Vatsiputriya
- Vibhajyavada
  - *Theravada
  - Mahishasaka
  - Dharmaguptaka
    - Vinaya School
      China: Lu-tsung
      Japan: Ritsu
- *Sarvastivada
  - Vaibhashika
  - Sautantrika
  - Satyasiddhi
    China: Ch'eng-shih
    Japan: Jojitsu
  - Kosha School
    China: Chushe
    Japan: Kusha

Chart 2: Mahayana

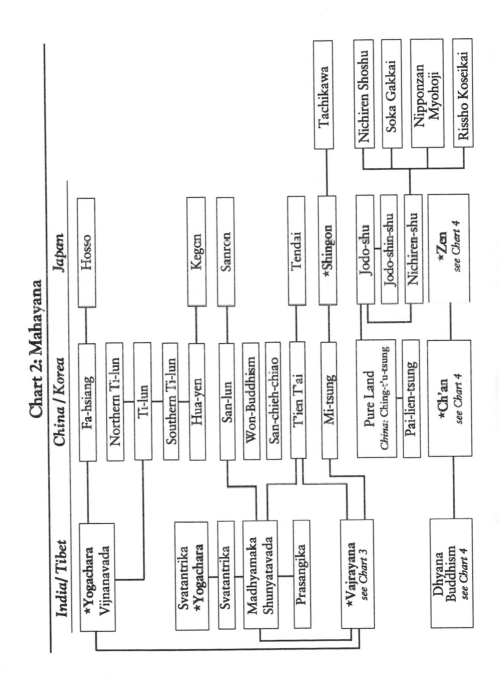

India/Tibet	China/Korea	Japan
*Yogachara Vijnanavada	Fa-hsiang	Hosso
	Northern Ti-lun	
	Ti-lun	
	Southern Ti-lun	
Svatantrika *Yogachara	Hua-yen	Kegon
Svatantrika	San-lun	Sanron
Madhyamaka Shunyatavada	Won-Buddhism	
	San-chieh-chiao	
Prasangika	T'ien T'ai	Tendai
	Mi-tsung	*Shingon
*Vajrayana see Chart 3	Pure Land *China:* Ching-t'u-tsung	Jodo-shu
		Jodo-shin-shu
	Pai-lien-tsung	Nichiren-shu
		Tachikawa
		Nichiren Shoshu
		Soka Gakkai
		Nipponzan Myohoji
		Rissho Koseikai
Dhyana Buddhism see Chart 4	*Ch'an see Chart 4	*Zen see Chart 4

Chart 3: Vajrayana

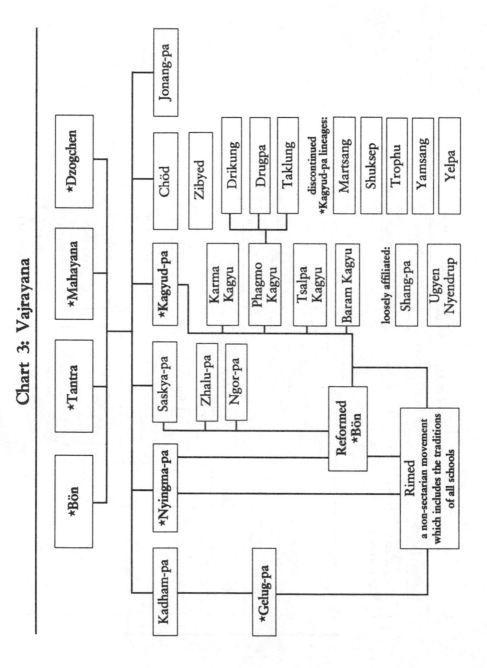

Chart 4: Ch'an/Zen

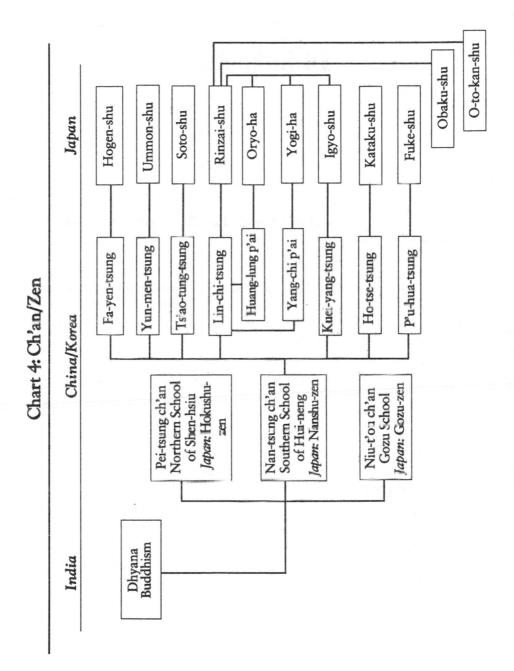

Bibliography

For translations of and additional literature pertinent to specific scriptures, see the relevant entry.

Allegro, John M. *The Dead Sea Scrolls: A Reappraisal.* 2nd ed. Harmondsworth, England: Penguin, 1964. Reprint 1982.

Baigent, Michael, and Richard Leigh. *The Dead Sea Scrolls Deception.* London: Jonathan Cape, 1991.

Banerjee, S. C. *see* Recommended Reading.

Beane, W. C. *Myth, Cult, and Symbols in Sakta Hinduism.* Leiden: Brill, 1977.

Branston, Brian. *Gods of the North.* London: Thames & Hudson, 1980.

Camphausen, Rufus C. *The History of Writing.* Amsterdam: Bres Magazine #144, 1990 (Dutch text).

———. *The Encyclopedia of Erotic Wisdom.* Rochester, Vt.: Inner Traditions, International, 1991.

Camphausen, Rufus C., and W. Winter, eds. *Bibliothek der Urschriften.* Uberlingen, Germany: W.Winter, 1982 (German book catalog).

Chan, Wing-tsit *see* Recommended Reading.

Dowman, Keith. *Masters of Mahamudra: Songs and Histories of the Eighty-Four Buddhist Siddhas.* Albany, New York: State University of New York Press, 1985.

Eliade, Mircea *see* Recommended Reading.

Farquhar, John N. *An Outline of the Religious Literature of India.* Delhi: Motilal, 1920.

Feuerstein, Georg. *Encyclopedic Dictionary of Yoga.* London: Unwin Hyman, 1990.

Fischer-Schreiber, Ingrid, et al., eds. *The Encyclopedia of Eastern Philosophy and Religion: Buddhism, Hinduism, Taoism, Zen.* Boston and London: Shambhala, 1988.

Graves, Robert, and Raphael Patai. *Hebrew Myths.* Garden City, N.Y.: Doubleday, 1964.

Gulik, Robert Hans van. *Sexual Life in Ancient China.* Leiden: Brill, 1961. Reprint 1974.

Kramer, Samuel Noah *see* Recommended Reading.

Lawlor, Robert. *Voices of the First Day: Awakening in the Aboriginal Dreamtime.* Rochester, Vt.: Inner Traditions International, 1991.

Meyer, Marvin W. *see* Recommended Reading.

Mitros, Joseph F. *Religions: A Select, Classified Bibliography.* New York: Learned Publications, 1973.

Snellgrove, David L., and Hugh Edward Richardson. *A Cultural History of Tibet.* Boulder: Prajna Press, 1968. Reprint 1980.

Strauss, Victor von. *Tao Te King* (in German). Zürich: Manesse, 1959.

Walker, Barbara G. *The Woman's Encyclopedia of Myths and Secrets.* San Francisco: Harper & Row, 1983.

Walker, Benjamin. *Tantrism: Its Secret Principles and Practices.* Wellingborough, England: Aquarian Press, 1982.

———. *Gnosticism: Its History and Influence.* Wellingborough, England: Aquarian Press, 1983.

Recommended Reading

Banerjee, S. C. *A Brief History of Tantra Literature*. Calcutta: Naya Prokash, 1988. A valuable work that provides information on almost one hundred Tantrik texts, many of which have not yet been translated. The author comments on the texts, gives historical informaton, and is generally less subjective than the perhaps better-known Farquhar (see Bibliography).

Chan, Wing-tsit, ed. and trans. *A Source Book in Chinese Philosophy*. Princeton, N.J.: Princeton University Press, 1963. Indispensable for the serious student of Chinese thought, this work embraces Confucian, Buddhist, and Taoist teachings and texts. A quality work with long quotes and sometimes complete translations of texts.

Eliade, Mircea. *From Primitives to Zen: A Thematic Sourcebook of the History of Religions*. London: Collins, 1967. Reprint 1983. A seductive collection of short extracts from most of the sacred scriptures that belong to *The Divine Library*—in fact, of more than are presented here. The book's strength is also its weakness: in attempting to be comprehensive, it can offer only very short pieces from everywhere in time and space. It does, however, belong in your library!

Kramer, Samuel Noah, ed. *Mythologies of the Ancient World*. Garden City, N.Y.: Doubleday, 1961. A wide-ranging work providing precise and concise information concerning the great classical cultures from around the world, with many quotations from the actual scriptures.

Meyer, Marvin W., ed. *The Ancient Mysteries: A Sourcebook*. San Francisco: Harper & Row, 1987. A unique collection of texts concerning the various mystery religions of the Mediterranean world, ranging from the Eleusinian mysteries to early Christianity and covering Greece, Anatolia, Rome, Egypt, and parts of the Near East.

Geographical / Cultural Index

Near East, Egypt, Persia

Tibet, Uddiyana and Zhang Zhung

Index of Scriptures

4. 在 青 天 者

5. 左 右 立

6.

上 古 結 縄
上 古 結 縄
上 古 結 繩
上 古 結 繩

b g d h f z ch t i k l m n s o p ts q

שית בָּרָא אֱלֹהִים אֵת הַשָּׁמַיִם וְאֵת הָאָרֶץ: וְהָאָרֶץ הָיְתָה תֹהוּ וְ

لفتى في العزّ مثل حياته و عيشة في الذلّ عين مماته

تى في العزّ مثل حياته و عيش في الذلّ عين ماته